RISK AN UNKNOWN FUTURE TO A KNOWN GOD

Risk an Unknown Future to a Known God

THE REWARDS OF FAITH IN GOD

BOSEDE NELSON

ARKJOY PRESS

Published in Manchester, UK by ARKJOY PRESS

Scripture quotations are taken from the Holy Bible obtained in Public domain: Unless otherwise denoted, scripture verses are taken from the following versions; King James Version, (KJV); New International Version (NIV) and New American Standard (NAS) Bible.

This book may be purchased in bulk for educational, business, fundraising, church activities or sales promotional use. For information, please e-mail ARKJOY.Press@gmail.com

Any person depicted on the cover of the page are being used for illustrative purposes only.

Given the dynamic nature of the internet, any web addresses or links in this book may have changed since publication and may no longer be valid.

ISBN 978-1-9993127-3-2

Printed in the United Kingdom

DEDICATION

To my heavenly Father, God:
To you, I give all the glory, honor and praise.

To my mother, Rowena:
I love and adore you. Thanks for your support over the years.

To my children, Olivia, Briana, and Jordanne:
I love and adore you. This book is part of a legacy of faith to
you.

CONTENTS

PART 3: LIVING THE VICTORIOUS LIFE

FOREWORD

*I*T HAS BEEN A DISTINCT PLEASURE TO KNOW MY sister in Christ, Bosede Nelson. She has been a great inspiration to me especially as I watched her faith-walk over the last couple of years. God is such an awesome and amazing God - omnipotent, omnipresent, and omniscient God. He loves and values us so much that He supplies all our needs, heals our diseases and is an ever-present help in times of trouble.

Bosede's faith-walk has given me a front row VIP seat, where I have had the privilege of peeking in the window of her vision and dream journey. This book shares the journey of a faithful and obedient family, standing on the promises of the Almighty God despite the trials and circumstances.

God bless you and your girls abundantly 'boss lady'! May you continue to share your walk to inspire and encourage those of us who need to make our journey in uncertain times. I can't wait for your next book! Readers you are in for a treat. Blessings to you all!

——Patricia Rose

*A*S FAR AS I CAN REMEMBER, MY MOTHER HAS been the backbone of our family, and through her, the Lord has truly blessed us. Her faith in God has always been inspirational. When we started the process of moving to the UK, not all things worked out as expected. It had me worried, but not my mom. She still believed and trusted God. It was almost as if she knew the outcome because she seemed unperturbed when trials and challenges nearly derailed our plans.

The transition from Jamaica to the UK was not smooth. It was one of the hardest things I've ever experienced. I lost hope multiple times, I doubted, and I questioned God. But listening to my mother's words of faith comforted me that things would get better. Although it was painful, stressful and draining, with my mom as a guide, I was able to build and renew my faith in God.

I am so grateful for what God has done in our lives. I now see opportunities that are bigger than anything I had ever imagined, and this is all due to my mother's obedience and faith in God. This experience has not only built my faith and love for God, but it has made me love and appreciate my mom even more. God has truly blessed my family, and with our continued faith in Him, we will always reap the rewards of His divine favor.

—Olivia Douglas

INTRODUCTION

THE DREAM CHASER

*"When we do business with people, we need
money. When we do business with God, we need
faith. Faith is the currency of the kingdom of
God."*[1]
- Reinhard Bonnke

*I*F SOMEONE HAD TOLD ME MY FUTURE WOULD
involve traveling on the road paved with heartache,
pain, and rejection and at the end was a great life full of
victory, I would say, "Forget it! Give me a comfortable life
instead." For years, I sought after a safe and comfortable
life. I acquired an education, found a relatively safe job, got
married, had three children and lived in a beautiful home
in Jamaica. Until I began to yearn for purpose in life; trying
to understand the reason for my existence and the kind of
legacy I wanted to leave my children. There was a void in
my life, and I couldn't shake the feeling for years. I tried

many things to suppress the void, but none of them worked until I decided to seek God for fulfillment. Many years have passed and oh! What an adventure it has been! Amidst life's challenges, the journey with God has been full of pleasant surprises and innumerable blessings.

God has often spoken to me through dreams either to respond to my prayers, to communicate His direction for my life or to warn me of impending danger. In early 2013, I received a series of dreams that marked the beginning of a radical shift in our lives, designed to catapult us into purpose. Guided by the interpretation of the dreams, we sold our possessions and left our family and friends behind to sojourned into an unknown land. God's plan unraveled in stages, but the path to get to the unknown destination was never revealed. The journey wasn't smooth. There were tremendous sacrifices, moments of heartache and pain, but through it all, God made us victorious! God rewarded our faith in Him! His blessings were double, triple and multiple folds! We are still flabbergasted by His goodness and mercy towards us. Looking back through the lens of my past, I can testify that despite adversities and challenges, victory is assured when you put your faith in God.

One of the things that inspired me to write our experience is that many people believe that faith in God as expressed in the Bible is a thing of the past, which cannot be replicated today. As a result, many people are stuck in their situation, afraid of believing God for greater things. After

THE DREAM CHASER

all, they seem to be doing well. They have the comforts of life – car, house, money, job, and family, yet deep down they are unhappy. Then there are others who aren't materially endowed but are also unhappy living beneath their potential. Whatever your situation is today, I encourage you to seek God and allow Him to break off the chains that are holding you back, and reach for your goals with faith, tenacity, and determination! God created you to be victorious in every area of your life, don't settle for less than God's best! You have one life to live, live it victoriously!

In this book, you will discover just how to do that! This book contains three parts that are designed to give you the tools to live a life of victory, overcome the challenges of this world, and accomplish the dreams God has placed within you. Contained within the pages of this book are the building blocks of faith in God. Biblical examples are used to set the context for each building block, and I recount our story of how we navigated each building block of faith and became victorious over every challenging situation.

As I take you through the pages of this book, it is my prayer that your faith in God will grow stronger and you too will be catapulted into purpose! I pray that as you put these twelve building blocks of faith into practice, your impossible situation will be made possible with God. God has a purpose for you, and it is designed to prosper and not to

xv

harm you, to give you hope, a bright future, and a victorious life! Why would you want to waste one single day living any other way? Why crawl when you can fly?

PART ONE

BECOMING A FAITH WARRIOR

CHAPTER ONE

SELF vs GOD:
THE CONCEPT OF FAITH

*"The only way you're going to reach places
you've never gone is if you trust God's direction
to do things you've never done."[2]*
— Germany Kent

*I*T IS QUITE NATURAL FOR PEOPLE TO SAY, "I HAVE
faith, and I believe for an expected outcome," whatever
that outcome may be. For example, airline passengers put
their confidence in the skills of a pilot to take them safely
to their destination, and patients put their trust in a doctor
for the right diagnosis and treatment. The truth is everyone has some measure of faith. The word 'faith' comes
from a Latin word *fidere*, which means to trust or believe.

The Oxford dictionary describes 'faith' (noun) as, *"complete trust or confidence in someone or something."*

For many years, I equated faith with self-confidence and having a positive outlook with strong determination and drive. I felt success in life was dependent on having these qualities. It wasn't until I experienced disappointments in areas of my life that I recognized that self-confidence was necessary but not enough to navigate life. I had limited control over life and its many uncertainties. Life felt like a roller coaster! One day I was up, the next day I was down. Each new day I opened with optimism and closed with doubt, fear, and anxiety. Something had to give! I couldn't continue living in this manner. I needed someone who was all-powerful, all-knowing, trustworthy, and faithful to help me navigate the future, and survive the inequities, disappointments, and tragedies of this world. It was therefore essential that I considered seriously whom I was putting my faith in, and whether the desired outcome would materialize.

THE BEGINNING OF MY FAITH JOURNEY

After years of navigating life on my own with limited interaction with God, there was a void in my life that marriage, children and career couldn't fill. I was unfulfilled and couldn't shake that feeling for several years. I was raised in a Christian home but had since departed the faith in my early twenties, living a life of partying and shacking up with my boyfriend who I later married.

I have three beautiful girls: Olivia, Briana, and Jordanne. When my eldest daughter, Olivia was in her early teens, I realized I had to radically shift gear in the way I was living to prevent my daughter from venturing down the same path I took. I began to seek the Lord on behalf of my children. I attempted to go to church, but the weight of caring for my family and pursuing my career trumped following God. It was not long after that the pedestal I placed my marriage tumbled down because of adultery. Attempts to reconcile proved futile and my marriage ended in divorce. The prospect of raising three children on my own, while experiencing the pain of separation almost drove me into depression. At this juncture, there was no one to run to with my pain except to God. I thank God for friends who attempted to help, but their help was insufficient. In my desperation, I made a deal with God that if He rescued my children and me, I would serve Him all the days of my life.

I made the first attempt by going to church regularly with my children and trusting God to take care of us. By reading God's Word consistently, I discovered the truth that without God, life is meaningless and a lack of trust and obedience to His Word means that life will be without ultimate significance, value, or purpose (Ecclesiastes 1:12-18). Soon after, I gave my life to God and got baptized.

Olivia followed in my footsteps, and so did Briana and Jordanne. I made a deal with God to rescue us, and He did!

Fourteen years have passed since I made that deal, and oh! What an adventure it has been! In retrospect, when I examine our lives, I recognize God has been ordering our footsteps all this time. He has closed some doors and opened others; He has brought people into our lives and removed others; He has warned us of impending danger and surprised us with unmerited favor. Psalm 37:23-24 tells us that, "The steps of a good man are ordered by the Lord: and he delights in his way. Though he falls, he shall not be utterly cast down: for the Lord upholds him with his hand."

God is indeed the master strategist and architect of our lives! We continue to reap the rewards of putting our faith in Him. In many instances, our blessings have been multiple folds as we trusted and followed His direction for our lives.

Now, I draw my self-confidence from being a child of the Almighty God. I don't have to worry about the future. I can risk putting my fate in God's hand, knowing that He holds the future and He has orchestrated my beginning and my end (Jeremiah 1:5). Putting my faith in God was the best decision I made! I am safe and secure in Him!

WHAT DOES IT MEAN TO HAVE FAITH IN GOD?

To have faith in God means to trust in Him wholeheartedly. He is the all-wise, all-knowing, all-powerful, gracious, merciful and loving God. In Him, you will find fulfillment no human being or thing can provide; you will have abundant life; and you will find grace, favor, love, forgiveness, protection, healing, joy, and eternal life. God loves and cares for us. His plans are perfect, holy, and righteous, and He works all things together for our good for those who love Him and are called according to His purpose (Romans 8:28).

Unlike human beings, God never lies, and He never fails to fulfill His promises. Numbers 23:19 tells us, "God is not a man, that He should lie, nor a son of man that He should change his mind. Does He speak and then not act? Does He promise and not fulfill?" God has the power to bring to pass whatever He plans to do. Isaiah 14:24 tells us, "The Lord Almighty has sworn, 'Surely, as I have planned, so it will be, and as I have purposed, so it will stand.'"

The Bible is full of many accounts of men and women who put their faith in God and were continually moving towards a higher calling. Throughout the Bible, the faith of the saints was never passive - but rather a faith of action, action which God met with His supernatural power to produce miraculous results! In Abraham's case, he heard the voice of God to leave his homeland and sojourn into a land that God would show him. God promised him a great name and blessings for him and his offspring. Abraham acted on his faith and risked an unknown future on God's command, and later birthed a new nation (Hebrews 11:8-10). Similarly, David acted on his faith, defeated Goliath, and later became the King of Israel (1 Samuel 17:1-48). God is Indeed a rewarder of faith!

Marcus Borg cites a metaphor used by Soren Kierkegaard, a great philosopher and radical Christian of the 19th century, who claimed that faith was like floating in a deep ocean. If we panic and struggle, Borg says, we will eventually sink. However, if we relax and trust, we will float, no matter how deep the water. Learning to relax in the water and let go of fear are keys to staying afloat in deep waters. Similarly, to have faith is to trust in God, to believe in God's ability to sustain us, to hold us up, even under challenging circumstances. Faith helps us to relax and let go, to rest and find peace.[3]

Faith in God is simple in form, yet its application is sometimes complicated because adults have challenges exercising their faith. Have you ever visited a friend's Facebook page and their relationship status reads, "it is complicated?" Yes indeed! This faith concept is quite similar; it is complicated for some adults. Children seem to grasp this concept unwittingly as they exercise total trust in their parents and God. Adults through pain, suffering, socialization, and disappointment in people, circumstances and life, sometimes believe it is pointless to trust in God.

I was at this crossroad some years ago, but I realized very quickly that life happens to everybody and, ".... the rain falls on the just and the unjust" (Mathew 5:45). Many of us have experienced pain, suffering, and tragedy, but no matter how hard or limited our understanding of the circumstances – be encouraged that God has our best interests at heart. For this reason, I decided to believe in an infinitely powerful and superior God instead of trying to navigate life all by myself.

Moreover, if we consider the alternative of trusting in ourselves or in others who are unpredictable, have limited wisdom and frequently make bad decisions, the choice should be obvious. Nevertheless, people fail to trust in God because they don't know Him. As a result, people become bound by anxiety or paralyzed by fear during times of uncertainty. "Do not worry about your life," Jesus tells us, "what you will eat or what you will drink... Look at the birds of the air; they neither sow nor reap nor gather into barns, and yet your heavenly Father feeds them. Are you not of more value than they?" (Matthew 6:25-26).

Are you anxious, worried or fearful today? Have faith in God! Trust God with your life, dreams, and aspirations. God is in your present, and your future as He was in your past. "Do not fear," says God in the words of the prophet

7

Isaiah, "for I have redeemed you; I have called you by name, you are mine. When you pass through the waters, I will be with you; and through the rivers, they shall not overwhelm you; when you walk through fire you shall not be burned, and the flame will not consume you... Do not fear, for I am with you" (Isaiah 43:1-5). I urge you today to trust God with your life, get to know God - to know God is to trust Him. May the Lord bless you richly!

CHAPTER TWO

HEARING WHEN GOD SPEAKS

"You must be positioned correctly in order to hear God speak."[4]
— Rick Warren

MOST OF MY UNSAVED FRIENDS DESERTED ME when I became a Christian because I was always talking about Jesus. The changes in my life were quite evident. As a young Christian, I started reading the Bible but preferred to watch Gospel television. I remember taking a nap one afternoon, and I heard a voice in my dream say, "Get up and look at the foot of your bed." I arose in my dream, looked at the foot of my bed and saw my Bible. The voice then said to me, "read it." I awoke out of my dream, raised myself from the bed, and to my amazement, the Bible was at the foot of the bed! From that moment, I started spending many hours reading the Bible.

There was another occasion when I awoke at about 2.00 am and decided to fold some clothes, including roughly twelve jeans. While I was folding the fourth jeans, I heard a quiet audible voice say, "Search the pockets." I considered the voice and decided to obey it. I searched the front pockets of the jeans – nothing! I searched the back pockets, and to my delight, I found 250 Jamaican dollars! I was entirely beside myself; I woke up my children to relay my experience to them. I went back to search the other jeans but didn't find anything else. The next day, I gave the money as an offering to the church.

Through past experiences, I have been able to discern the voice of God when He speaks. God continues to talk to me primarily through dreams and visions. He warns me of impending danger and provides direction when I don't seem to know how to navigate life's circumstances. I am sometimes inclined to consider myself a single parent raising three children, but I realize I am never alone. God is a Father to all of us; He speaks to us individually; He works in our lives as our provider, healer, protector, friend, savior, father, and King. To Him, I give all the glory, honor, and praise!

How To Hear From God

The Word of God is the foundation for our faith in God. Romans 10:17 says, "faith comes by hearing, and hearing by the Word of God." The first building block of our faith is to hear when God speaks. There are numerous accounts in the Bible of God speaking to individuals, to families, and to nations. He conversed with Adam in the Garden of Eden. He told Noah to build an ark. He spoke to Moses in a burning bush. He promised Abraham a son. Paul heard His voice on the road to Damascus. Through faith in God, they all obeyed His instructions.

You may ask, "How can I hear the voice of God?" God speaks in many ways. God speaks to all men (both women and men) through creation (Romans 1:18–20 and Psalm 19:1–2); through His written Word – the Bible; through angels (Luke 1:5–38); His prophets (II Samuel 24:10–25); dreams (Daniel 2:1–45); visions (Acts 9:10–18); miracles (Exodus 7:8–11); and even through a donkey that He enabled to speak as a man speaks! (Numbers 22:21–35.).

God also speaks in quiet moments (the still small voice) (1 Kings 19:11-14), and through life's circumstances (1 Samuel 1: 1-28). For example, through past experiences, I have observed how God answered my prayers and provided direction for my life, which has helped me to recognize His voice when He speaks to me in the present.

This kind of experience only comes through having a relationship with God, with continuous submission to Him and meditation on His Word.

HAVING A RELATIONSHIP WITH GOD

Hearing and obeying God's voice is conditional on having a relationship with Him. If you think about your relationships and consider the people you confide in, the voice you listen to and the advice you accept, I can assure you they are persons you trust. A relationship with God is quite similar but far superior. In this relationship, you will have an abundant life; you will find grace, favor, love, forgiveness, protection, healing, joy and eternal life with Him. There will never be a relationship in your life that's more important than the one with God through Jesus Christ. God is the perfect father, and He wants to have a relationship with you. Nothing compares to being a child of God.

A relationship with God can only begin by repenting of your sins and turning to Jesus Christ for salvation (being saved). Being saved is the precursor to having a real and genuine relationship with God (John 3:3). You may ask, "Why do I need to be saved?" The reason is that we cannot come into a relationship with a holy and perfect God in our natural state of sinfulness and our strength and morality (Romans 3:23).

Sin displeases God and separates us from Him. Every human being is born a sinner because of the sin of Adam and Eve which was passed down to all humanity (Gen 3:1-24). The payment for our sin is spiritual death - permanent separation from God. However, God sent His only son, Jesus Christ to die on the cross as payment for our sins and whosoever believes in Him shall be saved (John 3:16). You can only make things right with God through Jesus Christ, the Mediator between God and man (Romans 5:12). Therefore, you must be saved to enter into a relationship with a holy God.

Once saved, you need to become a student of the Word – the Bible, because this is the foundation of faith and life. Often the word you need to hear has already been written, and the Holy Spirit can bring it to your remembrance. The Holy Spirit is part of the Trinity, God in three persons – God, The father; God, the Son, and God, the Holy Spirit (John 14:26).

When the devil tempted Jesus (God, the Son) in the wilderness after fasting for 40 days and night, He quoted the Bible as a response to the devil (Luke4:1-13). It is therefore imperative that you read God's Word, so you can learn to recognize His voice, and can distinguish God's voice from other voices. Listening for God's voice without being dedicated to spending time in His Word on a regular basis opens you up to listening to voices in your mind or from other people that are not from God. Knowing the written Word protects you from deception.

DISTINGUISHING GOD'S VOICE

Over the course of your life, you will hear many voices that speak to you, either from people, or voices you hear in your mind. It is of utmost importance to verify those voices with God's written Word before you act. When God speaks, He will never contradict His written Word. His spoken Word may not be verbatim out of the Bible, but the principles are always supported in His written Word.

At times, people claim that God is telling them to do something that is in clear violation of His written Word. That is not the voice of God! For example, God will never lead you to suicide, fornication, adultery, stealing or murder, no matter what your situation is. It goes against His Word! God will never tell you to do something that His Word promises will lead to your destruction. He loves you way too much for that!

To protect yourself from deception, it is vital that you become a student of the Word. By continually reading and applying the Word to your life, you will begin to recognize when God speaks. For example, if you examine a newborn baby after several weeks of feeding on the mother's breast, the child knows her smell and her voice. If you give the baby to someone else, they often begin to cry because they are unfamiliar with that person. As far as the newborn baby is concerned, this person speaks, smells and acts differently from their mother.

In the same way, when you get saved, you become a newborn baby, who needs to feed on the Word of God continually. Spending time in His Word will enable you to recognize when God speaks and distinguish His voice from all other voices you may hear.

My prayer for you today is that you enter into a relationship with the Almighty God. Faith in God comes through a relationship with Him and becoming a student of His Word. The Christian life is built on a foundation of faith. "For by grace you have been saved through faith, and that not of yourself; it is the gift of God, not of works lest anyone should boast" (Ephesians 2:8).

Faith is also the basis for all progress into the unknown. Faith ventures into the unknown and unseen believing that there is more to reality than is presently known. Glenn Pease from Faith life Sermons uses imagery to explain faith and reasoning. He says, "faith is not opposed to reason, but it is faster than reason. It runs ahead, and lays hold on truths which reason is not yet capable of seeing. Reason travels by horse and buggy, while faith flies as fast as the speed of light-the light of God's Word and revelation. People of faith are always ahead of their time because they are continuously living based on truths that go beyond the best that reason and sight have developed."[5]

Today God is beckoning you to come into a relationship with Him just as you are. He has big dreams for you, a bright future and abundant life. I urge you to get to know God through His Word. You will never regret it!

CHAPTER THREE

THE SUBSTANCE OF THINGS WE DESIRE

"Never be afraid to trust an unknown future to
a known God."[6]
— Corrie ten Boom

*I*N THE PREVIOUS CHAPTERS, I DISCUSSED FAITH IN
God as trusting in Him wholeheartedly and obeying His
voice when He speaks. However, you may ask, "Why do I
need to do this?" As with all human beings, there will come
a time when you hope for something more, aspire for
something greater or merely doing something meaningful
with your life.

We all wonder why we are here on earth and often ask
ourselves, "What is the purpose of life?" Does this sound
familiar? If it does, I hope you take the time to consider the
questions below:

- What are you hoping for?
- Have you figured out what your purpose is?
- Do you know how to achieve the things you hope for?
- Are you happy with your success to date, or is there a void that remains unfilled?

If you are unsure of the answers to any of these questions, then press on reading to discover the things God accomplished in people who had faith in Him. Hebrews 11, often referred to as the faith chapter, gives an extensive exposition of people who heard the voice of God, trusted and obeyed His instructions. Some received the reward of faith in their lifetime; others, generations after. The Bible says:

> *Now faith is the substance of things hoped for, the evidence of things not seen. For by it the elders obtained a good report.*
>
> — Hebrews 11:12 (KJV)

The first part of the scripture verse says, "faith is the substance of things hoped for...." The word "substance" is translated as "assurance" by the *American Standard Version* (ASV) of the Bible and defined *as* "a standing under or support." Faith is, therefore, the assurance for our hope; it stands under and supports our hope. Thus, our hope is only as secure as the strength of our faith.[7]

The second part of the verse says, ".... faith is the evidence of things not seen," with "evidence" translated as "conviction" by the ASV or proof or proving. Thus, faith is not based on feelings or emotions; it is a conviction supported by evidence. [8] In essence, believing God is the assurance for the things hoped for and trusting God is proof of things not seen.

I like to simplify this scripture verse by saying, "I believe God based on evidence in His Word which provides me with the assurance that the things I hope for will materialize even though I cannot see how, when and where it will occur." Sight is therefore irrelevant for hope. If you can see it with the natural eye, then there is no need to hope for it. Hebrews 11:4 also says:

> *But without faith it is impossible to please him:*
> *for He that cometh to God must believe that He*
> *is and that He is a rewarder of them that dili-*
> *gently seek Him.*
>
> - Hebrews 11:4 (KJV)

In this verse, faith includes two elements: First, it is a conviction of truth. We "must believe that He is." Second, it is a statement of trust. We "must believe ... that He is a rewarder of them that diligently seek Him." Conviction causes us to accept His Word and trust leads us to obey

Him.[9] God rewards those who have faith in Him and seek after Him diligently.

Tracing the lineage of Abraham to Jesus (Mathew 1:17) demonstrates a family that lived by faith – faith in God. Hebrews 11: 8-10 tells us that, "By faith Abraham, when he was called to go out into a place which he should after receive for an inheritance, obeyed; and he went out, not knowing where he went. By faith, he sojourned in the land of promise, as in a strange country, dwelling in taber-nacles with Isaac and Jacob, the heirs with him of the same promise. For he looked for a city which hath foundation, whose builder and maker is God."

Abraham's faith in God was the assurance that his hope of finding this city will materialize even though when he obeyed the voice of God, he didn't know where he was going. His act of obedience not only pleased God, but God rewarded him for it.

MIGRATION PLANS REVEALED THROUGH DREAMS

Quite like Abraham's sojourn into an unknown land, the Lord called my children and me out of Jamaica to venture into new territory. Before this, I was hoping for a better life for myself, better prospects for my children, companion-ship and a deeper relationship with God. Simply put, I was asking God to enlarge my territory! God heard my prayers.

The instructions from God to leave Jamaica came through several dreams, each one giving a glimpse of the destination, but the journey was unknown. As we took the first step to obey God, the plan of the Lord began to unravel in stages, but the path to get to the unknown land wasn't revealed. Just as the ten lepers in Luke 17:11-19 who, after crying out for mercy, Jesus told them to go and show themselves to the priests. As they went, they were cleansed from leprosy. Similarly, as we walked in obedience, and in line with the interpretation of the dreams, the Lord gradually unfolded the plans.

First Dream

The Lord has often spoken to me through dreams. My first dream which signaled the beginning of a life-changing event occurred in 2013. In the dream, I saw myself driving an open back truck full of lots of stuff covered in the back of the truck. I had stopped and left the engine running when an elderly lady affectionately known as 'Storyteller Clarke' from my Church brought me some plantains. I distinctly remember pondering where I was going to put the plantains considering the truck was full. She insisted, and I told her I would call my daughter Olivia to arrange for extra suitcases to put the additional stuff. While I was trying to fit the plantains in the back of the truck, I looked up and saw my friend Tina who resides in Canada, walking in front of the truck. She curiously looked at the truck and then continued on her way.

I awoke from the dream somewhat perplexed but recognized I was traveling somewhere but didn't know where I was going. One thing was sure; it was not Canada!

Second Dream

Some days later, I received a second dream. Some members of my church came to my house for a sleepover. A few church members arose early the next day because I insisted on leaving on time to catch my flight. Other church members were tired and decided not to escort me. For those who were willing, I had a bus waiting to take them to a location. We ate, socialized and had a wonderful time at the place. I was speaking with Olivia, when a church member came across to join us, pulling a trolley with a carton of milk and some snacks. He sat between Olivia and me and was muttering something which made her laugh. Shortly after, I signaled my departure and informed them about the car waiting for me around the corner.

I awoke from the dream, and my spirit was disturbed. I pondered again where the Lord was taking me. It seemed I was going without my children and the prospect frightened me. I noted from the dream, however, that Olivia was not sad, so I took comfort in the knowledge that where I was going didn't bring grief but happiness to her.

INTERPRETATION OF DREAMS

As a routine, I seek God in prayer immediately after experiencing dreams, mindful of the fact that not all dreams come from God. I prayed for the interpretation of these two dreams, and the Holy Spirit brought to my remembrance the story of Joseph in the Bible. From this revelation, three crucial lessons aided my interpretation and response to the dreams.

The first lesson came from Genesis 40:8, where Joseph acknowledged that God is the interpreter of dreams. When Joseph was called upon to interpret Pharaoh's two dreams, Joseph said to Pharaoh:

> *It is not in me: God shall give Pharaoh an answer of peace. The dream of Pharaoh is one: God hath shewed Pharaoh what he is about to do.*
> - Genesis 41:16, 25 (KJV)

Using this interpretation, I recognized that both my dreams were one and God was showing me what He was about to do. The second lesson came from Joseph's response to Pharaoh's dream:

The dream was doubled unto Pharaoh twice; it is
because the thing is established by God, and God
will shortly bring it to pass.

- Genesis 41:32 (KJV)

In applying God's written Word, I knew clearly that my
two dreams were one, established by God and will shortly
come to pass. The third lesson was merely to remain silent
about the dreams and not make the mistake Joseph did
when he told his brothers about his dreams:

Then Joseph had a dream, and when he told it to
his brothers, they hated him even more. He said
to them, "Please listen to this dream which I have
had; for behold, we were binding sheaves in the
field, and lo, my sheaf rose up and also stood
erect; and behold, your sheaves gathered around
and bowed down to my sheaf." Then his brothers
said to him, "Are you actually going to reign over
us? Or are you really going to rule over us?" So
they hated him even more for his dreams and for
his words. Now he had still another dream, and
related it to his brothers, and said, "Lo, I have
had still another dream; and behold, the sun and
the moon and eleven stars were bowing down to

me." He related it to his father and to his broth-
ers; and his father rebuked him and said to him,
"What is this dream that you have had? Shall I
and your mother and your brothers actually
come to bow ourselves down before you to the
ground?" His brothers were jealous of him, but
his father kept the saying in mind.

- Genesis 37: 5-11(NAS)

There are times when you experience profound dreams or visions. Guard your mouth not merely because people might hate you for your dreams, but they may infuse doubt or sow seeds of negativity. This negativity may eventually cast doubt and unbelief in your mind and destroy your faith while it is at its formative stages. I have learned that when God is performing a mighty work in my life, I can't share the information with everyone. Some persons will not be happy to hear your story. The lesson is to know when to speak, what to say or when to remain silent. I chose to stay silent.

It would have been wonderful to say that with all my application of Bible knowledge, I instantly rejoiced knowing I was about to begin a new chapter in my life. Quite the contrary, I was full of trepidation. I wondered how this dream was going to be accomplished. I thought about the original plans I had to stay in Jamaica. I thought about leaving friends and family behind and the life we had built, and

I was scared. My response was to prove I unequivocally heard God speak before acting. I did something quite akin to what Gideon did in Judges 6:36-40. I asked God for confirmation of these dreams.

> Then Gideon said to God, "If You will deliver Israel through me, as You have spoken, behold, I will put a fleece of wool on the threshing floor. If there is dew on the fleece only, and it is dry on all the ground, then I will know that You will deliver Israel through me, as You have spoken." And it was so. When he arose early the next morning and squeezed the fleece, he drained the dew from the fleece, a bowl full of water. Then Gideon said to God, "Do not let Your anger burn against me that I may speak once more; please let me make a test once more with the fleece, let it now be dry only on the fleece, and let there be dew on all the ground." God did so that night; for it was dry only on the fleece, and dew was on all the ground.
>
> - Judges 6:36-40 (NAS)

Third Dream

Some days later, I had a dream with two parts. In the first part, my co-workers visited my house. Strangely in the dream, my house was empty. I saw all the familiar faces except for my friend, Tom whom I thought would have been the first person to arrive at my home. In the second part of the dream, I saw myself eavesdropping on Tom's conversation, and overheard him saying he will see us in the next two years. I replied saying that you may not see us for quite a while. Afterward, I left my co-workers at my house and hurried to a store to purchase two pencils. I got impatient with the store owner for moving sluggishly, informing him that I was in a hurry to catch my flight.

I arose from the dream, having the confirmation I needed from God. Each dream also gave me further clues, such as the suitcase, the flight, the empty house, and the pencils. The empty house I figured was migration, not merely a two-year visit. I pondered on the pencils for a while and considered whether I was going away to study.

A troubling aspect of my dreams was the absence of my children except for Olivia, who appeared in two of the three dreams. I weighed the prospect of leaving my children and decided it was not an option. Alternatively, I considered whether the decision to migrate mainly affected myself and Olivia, which may have explained the absence of my other two children in the dreams. Albeit, I informed my children and my friend, Patricia about my dreams while I enquired of the Lord and waited on Him to reveal the next steps.

WAITING ON THE LORD

Waiting on God means we are alert, listening, and ready to obey His command. Abraham exemplified the meaning of waiting on the Lord. First, God gave him general promises about a future blessing. As he sojourned out of his comfort zone and arrived in Canaan, God reaffirmed His promise and gave him more details, "To your offspring, I will give this land" (Genesis12:7). Throughout the rest of Abraham's story, the promises continued to unfold in more specific dimensions as Abraham journeyed through the land.

It is crucial to wait on the Lord as Isaiah 40:31 says, "But they that wait upon the Lord shall renew their strength; they shall mount up with wings as eagles; they shall run, and not be weary, and they shall walk, and not faint."

Sometimes we get excited about what God is doing in our lives that we want to grab hold of the reins and run the program ourselves. We must remember that God's timing is best and doing something before the season may circumvent the entire process. Therefore, my friend, I urge you to wait on the Lord!

CHAPTER FOUR

FAITH WITHOUT ACTION IS DEAD

"God always works with workers and moves with movers, but He does not sit with sitters."[10]
— *Reinhard Bonnke*

I KNEW GOD ESTABLISHED MY DREAMS BECAUSE I aligned them to His Word and received confirmation. In response to the interpretation of the dreams aided by the Holy Spirit, I decided to do two things to put my faith into action; I began purchasing suitcases and bags in line with the interpretation of the first dream, where I needed extra suitcases to put the additional stuff.

Secondly, I stopped buying work attire based on my understanding of the third dream where I saw myself purchasing pencils. I surmised that I was going to pursue further studies and wouldn't need work attire but casual clothes. All I knew was I was traveling somewhere, not for a two-year visit but more permanently.

OUR FAITH IN ACTION

I was still unsure of the Lord's direction, even though I had begun to put my faith into action. These were scary times for us, mainly because these changes meant significant shifts in our lives. During the period, Olivia was in the process of her university applications. We initially applied to the local university and received acceptance, but we felt the direction wasn't aligned with the dreams. By deduction, we began applying to universities in the UK.

We surmised that Canada was not an option given the first dream. The USA was ruled out because of its lengthy migration process, contrary to the interpretation that the dreams would come through shortly. Therefore, we felt it was the UK given our British citizenship status. Olivia then began her applications to UK universities. She also pursued extra courses to improve her chances of obtaining part-time jobs while attending university.

Concurrently, Jordanne, my youngest daughter had just completed the Grade Six Achievement Test (GSAT) and was awaiting the results which would determine her secondary school placement. Briana, my second daughter, had just entered lower six-form and was skeptical of the implications of these dreams for schooling, friends and extended family. All my children were at a critical point in their academic pursuit, and although the changes appeared frightening, we pressed ahead!

At work, I decided to expedite all outstanding assignments and began cleaning out my office and getting rid of the junk I had accumulated over the years. I abstained from attending any overseas course considering the company's one-year bonding policy, which meant breaking the bond before expiration would require full repayment.

It was preparation time for us! I remember attending a local risk management course. Afterward, I spoke to the facilitator of the course about further studies in risk management or finance. He encouraged me to consider a post-graduate degree (Doctor of Philosophy (PhD)), and He discussed several options for funding including scholarships. When he learned of my British citizenship, he conveyed that he knew several persons who had obtained a commonwealth scholarship to pursue a PhD in the UK.

Unbeknown to him, he unlocked the door to a serious consideration of a PhD program. With continued prayer for the correct interpretation of the two pencils in my third dream, and armed with the knowledge of the PhD pathway, I began my university and commonwealth scholarship applications.

Some UK universities require the submission of the results of the Graduate Record Examination (GRE) as part of their entry requirements. It was one of my most difficult exams, probably because of the short timeframe I had to sit the exam or miss enrolment into several universities altogether. I spent several hours studying at night. On exam day, I didn't feel adequately prepared, but God favored me! I was tested on the areas I gave full coverage, and I was successful.

Another university requirement was to complete a PhD proposal (i.e., selecting an original topic, reviewing the literature, providing the methodology and expected results). I was up early most mornings trying to complete my proposal, while still holding a day job, driving my children to school and picking them up after school. These were difficult and frustrating times, but we pressed ahead nonetheless. I prayed fervently! I knew my strength couldn't sustain me. I needed strength from the Lord to follow His direction for our lives. I completed my proposal; armed with my GRE results, I applied to several UK universities and for the commonwealth scholarship. I prayed, waited on the Lord for further instructions and acted on those instructions when they came.

ARE YOUR ACTIONS EVIDENT?

Many people say they have faith and believe in God's Word, but then what? What comes next? For example, if you have faith that God will heal you and you believe God for that healing, how have your actions demonstrated your faith in God? The Bible expounds on this concept of demonstrated action:

> *What use is it, my brethren, if someone says he has faith, but he has no works? Can that faith save him? If a brother or sister is without clothing and in need of daily food, and one of you says to them, "Go in peace, be warmed and be filled," and yet you do not give them what is necessary for their body, what use is that? Even so faith, if it has no works, is dead, being by itself. 26For just as the body without the spirit is dead, so also faith without works is dead.*
>
> - James 2:14 -17, 26 (NAS)

James tells us that corresponding action must accompany faith; otherwise, it is dead. A better word for 'dead' might be 'dormant,' or 'inoperative.' Actions are needed to bring faith to life. Thus, we must act on our belief with actions or works consistent with what we believe.

THE BELIEVER'S FAITH IN ACTION

Throughout the Bible, the faith of the saints was never passive - but rather a faith of action, action which God met with His supernatural power to produce fantastic, miraculous and astounding results. In Mathew 14:29, Peter received faith to walk on water when he heard Jesus say, 'Come.' However, that faith did not come alive until he threw his leg over the side of the boat, stepped on the water and started walking. Thus, Peter's action unlocked the power resident in faith.[11]

In Abraham's case, he heard the voice of God to leave his homeland and sojourn into a land that God would show him. God promised remarkable things for his future: a great name, protection, and blessing for him and his offspring. Abraham acted on his faith, packed up his family and belongings and went just as the Lord had told him, willing to risk an unknown future on God's command. If Abraham had never acted on his faith, He would never have departed to the "land of milk and honey" or birthed a new nation. Similarly, if Moses had never acted on his faith, he would never have led the children of Israel out of Egypt. If David had never moved on his faith, He would never have defeated Goliath nor become the King of Israel. God is Indeed a rewarder of faith![12] The most important thing to learn as you build your faith in God is to obey His every command and act on His Word.

Everyone then who hears these words of mine and acts on them will be like a wise man who built his house on a rock. The rain fell, the floods came, and the winds blew and beat on that house, but it did not fall, because it had been founded on a rock. And everyone who hears these words of mine and does not act on them will be like a foolish man who built his house on sand. The rain fell, and the floods came, and the winds blew and beat against that house, and it fell--and great was its fall!

- Matthew 7:24-27 (NIV)

These dramatic words of Jesus emphasized action. Matthew didn't doubt that acting on what Jesus said was tantamount to doing the will of God. On this life journey, God is always directing our footsteps through both good and bad times. It may all seem like a huge jigsaw puzzle. Some things happen in our lives that we may never understand. For some of us, it is when we retrospectively examine our lives we see how God has ordered our footsteps.

We never know how the things we hope for are going to materialize, but God does! He alone knows the end from the beginning. Therefore, it is vital that we put our trust in Him. I asked you at the beginning of Chapter 3, "What is the purpose of life?" I hope your answer will now be, "to do the will of God, by obeying and acting on His every instruction to me" (Ecclesiastes12:13).

Today I urge you to trust in God and let your faith fuel your actions, and most assuredly this will be a new day of miracles, breakthroughs, and victory - for a life of faith, is a life of victory!

~PART TWO~

OVERCOMING TRIALS AND TRIBULATIONS

CHAPTER FIVE

TRUE FAITH IS TRIED AND TESTED

"Here is the great secret of success. Work with all your might; but trust not in the least in your work. Pray with all your might for the blessing of God; but work, at the same time, with all diligence, with all patience, with all perseverance. The result will surely be, abundant blessing."[13]
— *George Muller*

THERE IS AN OLD SAYING IN JAMAICA THAT, "wen yuh want gud, yuh nose affi run." Translating from the vernacular, it means, "nothing good comes easy." True faith is tried and tested. True faith is not moved by what is seen but is resolute and determined to obey God regardless of the situation. The people in the Bible that accomplished great feats for God went through testing - their faith was tested. James 1:4 puts it like this:

> *My brethren count it all joy when ye fall into divers temptations. Knowing this, that the trying of your faith worketh patience. But let faith have her perfect work, that ye may be perfect and entire, wanting nothing.*
>
> - James 1:4 (KJV)

The verse tells us that during times of trouble (divers' temptations), our attitude should be one of joy as it represents an opportunity for our faith to work and for God to achieve the victory through us.

The second part of the verse says, ".... the trying of your faith worketh patience." The word "patience" is equated with the quiet assurance that when tested, faith in the life of a person committed to obeying God produces an inevitable victory![14]

Patience has two elements: perseverance and persistence. Perseverance is the ability to endure the storm, without being washed overboard but persistence goes beyond perseverance. Perseverance only seeks to survive the storm, while persistence proceeds toward doing the will of God despite the storm. [15]

The reality is that we don't always enter trials with patience. Most of us start with faith alone but come out with faith and patience. Job in the Bible didn't begin his trial with patience. He began with unwavering trust in God. Even though we know him as a great man of patience, he didn't have patience at the start of his trials but acquired it by the end. We know he didn't have it because he spent considerable time frustrated with his friends, his wife and with himself. During his trial, he came to grips with some truths about himself, God and life generally and came forth out of his trial with a renewed faith and trust in God. When he came forth, Job was a man of patience (Job 42).[16]

Has your faith ever been tested? Has there ever been a time when you felt challenged by a series of circumstances? What was your response? The ideal reaction to challenging moments is to approach them with confidence, endure them with courage, and arise from them with an even stronger faith in God.[17]

IN THE LINE OF FIRE!

There were many instances when trials and challenges tested our faith in God. For example, Jordanne, my youngest daughter was awaiting her GSAT results which would determine her secondary school placement. Before the exams, parents were required to select five schools and rank them by preference. I chose the top five schools in Jamaica, listed them in the same order for all my three children. Moreover, Jordanne would only attend secondary school for one year before migrating. I surmised she needed to get into one of the top schools to ensure a smooth transition into UK schools. I believed God for an excellent school for her. However, when the results were released, Jordanne didn't get into any of the five selections, and I didn't consider the school she was placed very highly.

Similarly, Olivia had applied to five UK universities, and all five universities rejected her application. She was placed in the next round of selection when extra spaces became available. These were trying times. Feelings of discouragement, disappointment, and rejection were running a mock during this period. However, we declared and stood on the promises of God that "......no good thing will he withhold from them that walk uprightly" (Psalm 84:11).

Amidst the chaos, the governing body for the commonwealth scholarship rejected my application. I had applied to eleven universities over the period, and the rejection letters slowly trickled in four months before leaving Jamaica. I received ten rejection letters, awaiting the final university – The University of Manchester.

While I awaited the last university, I heard the Lord say that I should speak with my boss and inform her of my plans. Again, I enquired of the Lord about the plans, considering we had no university offers in hand. The next day

I was apprehensive; my boss realized something was wrong. She invited me into her office, and I told her about my plans to pursue further studies in the UK without giving any definitive answer to her questions.

I was extremely uncomfortable signaling my impending move without being able to offer any details. Nevertheless, I obeyed God's instructions. My boss provided some options concerning work and study and the requirements to apply for study-leave. She advised that if my route was study-leave, my application should have been submitted already. Given the late notice, she advised me to speak with the head of the area about my plans and afterward, submit my study-leave application by the next day. I wasn't quite sure what route to take regarding funding my education, but I decided to heed her advice.

Can you imagine my trepidation? I had no offer in hand, yet I had to speak with the head of the area and apply for study-leave the next day. I was beside myself! I cried out to the Lord in prayer to show me in clear terms where we were going. Around 2.00 am the following day, I arose to check my email, and to my excitement, I received an offer from the University of Manchester, to pursue a one-year master's degree and upon successful completion to enter the three-year PhD program. Oh hallelujah! Glory to God! He answered my prayers! I was now able to speak with the head of the area at 9.00 am confirming my plans to pursue further studies in the UK. Oh, what a victory!

Even though it was difficult, I obeyed God's instructions, and He rewarded me for it. God is indeed an on-time God!

KEYS TO DEVELOPING PATIENCE DURING TRIALS

I articulated at the beginning of this chapter that the testing of our faith works patience. The Bible makes it clear that there can be no patience gained without trials endured. There can be no victory unless there is a battle. [18]

Now, how can you develop the quiet assurance that it is well in your life? Moreover, how can you acquire patience? The keys to obtaining patience during trials are to endure small storms and never lose sight of your goal while gaining strength for more significant storms that will come. Those who exemplified great faith in the Bible were those who entered a troubling situation with confidence that it cannot overwhelm them, cannot frighten them and will not break their resolve to proceed towards their goal.[19]

If you ask Daniel (Daniel 6:6-21), he will tell you that you may pray all day long. However, you don't know that the Lord will answer your prayer until you have been in the Lion's Den. When you have faced the growling fangs of death and been in the grasp of adversity and watched the Lord quiet down angry lions, only then can you say, "I know the Lord will answer prayer for I have tried him for myself." If you ask the three Hebrew Boys (Daniel 3:19-26), they will tell you that you may believe that God can deliver you, but you don't know that the Lord will deliver you until you have been in the fiery furnace. When you feel the heat of opposition, burning seven times hotter than it normally burns. When you feel the protective arms of God surround you and you hear the voice of the world ask, "didn't we put three men in the fire, behold I see four, and the fourth man looks like the son of God," then you can say God delivers because you have proven God for yourself! [20]

When challenges try your faith, it reveals the depths of your conviction. "Did you believe God in the first place and despite the adversity, setbacks, and disappointments, will your faith still hold strong?" Abraham's faith was severely tested when in Genesis 22:1-13, he was told by God to sacrifice his son, the son of promise. His response was to do according to what God said because he reckoned that God who gave the promise could raise his son from the dead.

There are many others in the Bible where trials tested their faith in different ways. Some in seemingly small ways, while others in huge ways. It, therefore, boils down to the question, "Did you believe God?" "You say you do, but when the time comes for you to demonstrate your belief, do you quibble, hide or give up?" Recall the part of the definition of faith, which says, "....... the evidence of things not seen." "Does it mean, therefore, that you give up and stop trusting God because you have not seen the promise?" or "what you have seen is contrary to what was promised?" In these situations, you should ask yourself, "Whose report am I going to believe?" Our collective response should be, "We shall certainly believe the report of the Lord!"

Your situation will be different, but the principles are applicable. You may have received a negative report about your health, your finances, your job or your family and friends, but I dare you to trust and obey God. Put your faith into action and persevere. God is still in the miracle-working business. The same God that was in the lion's den with Daniel; that same God is with us today – Jesus Christ, who died on Calvary and arose on the third day! He was tried in the fire! He came forth as fine gold, resurrected and seated at the right hand of the Father (Acts 2:33).

Likewise, the next time your faith is tried and tested, you too can come forth as pure gold. When you have won the victory through Jesus, you can shout that God is indeed a deliverer! From my story, I have the evidence to shout that God is my deliverer! He is my way maker!

I urge you to continue to resolve and face every difficulty that life presents with confidence and optimism that God will work all things to your advantage in His time and in His supernatural way. After all, "We know that all things work together for good to them that love God, to them who are called according to His purposes (Romans 8:28).

Have you been tried in the fire? Did you...Did you come forth as pure gold?[21]

CHAPTER SIX

MUSTARD SEED FAITH CAN MOVE MOUNTAINS

"Faith talks in the language of God. Doubt talks in the language of man."[22]
— *E.W Kenyon (Pastor)*

*I*N CHAPTER FIVE, I STARTED TELLING YOU THE STORY about Jordanne's unexpected GSAT results. Well, let me retrace my steps somewhat and give you the entire story. As it was customary for me, I wrote the vision for Jordanne's results before the exam, and I prayed, worked hard with her, and left the rest to God. In fact, the Bible tells us to write the vision in Habakkuk 2:

> And the Lord answered me, and said, write the vision, and make it plain upon tables, that he may run that readeth it. For the vision is yet for

an appointed time, but at the end it shall speak,
and not lie: though it tarry, wait for it; because it
will surely come, it will not tarry.

- Habakkuk 2:2- 3(KJV)

I wrote the vision and made it plain for Jordanne as I did for my other two daughters. The vision was for her to attend the highest ranked secondary school in Jamaica with a government scholarship. Parents were required to indicate their five secondary school selections on a form, which was then submitted to the governing body, the Ministry of Education. I listed the same choices, in the same order for all my children. When the GSAT results were released, Jordanne wasn't selected for any of her five choices.

Upon hearing her placement, I was utterly shocked and dismayed. I was resolute she wasn't going to attend the school she was placed given its poor reputation. I wanted her to attend an excellent school to make the transition to the UK easier. Many people tried to convince me that the school she was placed was a good school. They indicated that with her eighty-five percent average GSAT result, Jordanne wouldn't have received offers into any of the five selections given the stiff competition.

"What do you do when the report or results are not as expected?" I wondered what could have possibly gone wrong. I prayed earnestly, worked hard with her, but her grades did not place her in any of her choices. Nevertheless, after I recovered from the shock, I began the process of applying for transfer into one of the five schools that we originally selected. However, two of those schools indicated they wouldn't accept any transfers; this left us with three schools. Jordanne later informed me that she didn't want to attend the schools her sisters previously attended (the top two of the five schools) because she craved her independence. We were left with one school – a highly ranked secondary school for girls.

I rushed over to the school to request a transfer, only to be told by the Principal that all transfers were closed. I gave her my transfer letter. She took a cursory glance at it and told me it would take a miracle for Jordanne to get into the school. I responded with a smile and said, "I serve a miracle working God."

I continued to pray earnestly, and the Lord gave me a word, "faith without works is dead." That was all I needed to hear. On registration day, Jordanne and I went to the school. Parents whose children were accepted were required to join a queue and pick up their child's package and then proceed into the main hall for an introductory meeting. We could not join the line, considering Jordanne had no offer, but instead we went into the main hall and sat with the rest of the parents. Everyone had a package, but we didn't. We sat through the meeting that lasted over three hours.

Afterward, I spoke to both the Principal and the Vice-principal, gave them my business card and informed them I was enrolling Jordanne into their summer school program. On my way out of the school's office, the Vice-principal beckoned to me and said she admired my faith and I should continue to persevere. Now isn't that God confirming His word through this lady! I felt so encouraged.

While I anxiously awaited their decision, I took the opportunity to send an email to the Principal beseeching her to reconsider my transfer request. I also presented myself at the school almost every week during the summer. Moreover, Jordanne and I agreed that we would only speak in line with our belief. When anyone asked about her school placement, our collective response was – "the highly ranked secondary school for girls."

In the meantime, I was adamant I wasn't going to pay a registration fee to the school she was initially accepted. The registration fee was required to secure her space. As far as we were concerned, the highly ranked secondary school for girls was our school of choice, disciplined with strong Christian values. On my fifth appearance at the school, the Principal, who was now familiar with my face told me to expect a call regarding the outcome of the decision. I didn't know when she would call, but I had decided I was going ahead to purchase her school uniforms that Saturday.

MUSTARD SEED FAITH CAN MOVE MOUNTAINS

I went on a three day fast and solicited agreement in prayer with family members and friends. Mathew 18:19-20 tells us that, ".... if two of you on earth agree about anything they ask for, it will be done for them by my Father in heaven. For where two or three are gathered in my name, there am I with them." We prayed and agreed that the Lord would imprint Jordanne's name on the Principal's mind.

Well, the conclusion of the matter was the Principal called that Saturday morning and said she couldn't get Jordanne's name off her mind; therefore, they decided to create a space for her at the School. The Principal said she felt compelled to do so because "You just kept coming back." In keeping with our original plan, we went ahead with joy in our hearts and purchased the full set of uniforms that Saturday afternoon. Glory to God! Yet another victory!

MUSTARD SEED FAITH WORKS

The moral of my story is that even if your faith is as small as a mustard seed, you can move mountains. However, some people believe their faith is not resilient enough to endure hard trials. There is no truth in that statement! It is not the quantity of your faith that matters but the quality. Jesus said, "If ye have faith as a grain of mustard seed, ye shall say unto this mountain, remove hence to yonder place; and it shall remove; and nothing shall be impossible unto you" (Matthew 17:20).

A mustard seed is a tiny seed that carries within itself the DNA of the parent plant. With adequate nutrients, a mustard seed will grow into a mustard plant, and the plant will then grow to a remarkable size in comparison to the seed.[23] Jesus used the mustard seed to illustrate the principles of the Kingdom of God in several ways:

- First, the analogy portrays faith (which comes from hearing the word of God) as a living thing (seed) that grows within us to produce remarkable things;
- Second, the mustard seed carries the DNA of the parent plant, so our faith carries the DNA of Jesus, who is the author and finisher of our faith (Hebrew 12:2): and
- Third, the quantity of our faith is irrelevant to move mountains, but the quality of our faith in God is crucial.[24]

You don't need to increase your faith to do God's will; you need a pure faith (no doubt or unbelief), the size of a grain of mustard seed to move mountains and do the impossible. You can speak to the mountains in your life today, and they shall be removed because you are a believer and not a doubter. Jesus said:

Verily, verily, I say unto you, He that believeth on me, the works that I do shall he do also; and greater works than these shall he do; because I go unto my Father.

- John 14:12(KJV)

The Bible bears witness to many people who had both small and big faith. Let's examine the story of Joshua and the fight with the Amorites:

On the day the LORD gave the Amorites over to the Israelites, Joshua spoke to the LORD in the presence of Israel:" Sun, stand still over Gibeon, and moon, over the Valley of Aijalon." So the sun stood still, and the moon stopped, till the nation avenged itself on its enemies, as it is written in the Book of Jashar. There was no day like that before it or after it, when the LORD listened to the voice of a man; for the LORD fought for Israel. Then Joshua and all Israel with him returned to the camp to Gilgal.

- Joshua 10:13-14(KJV)

Talk about Faith! What a reward from God! The Bible says God listened to the voice of man and allowed the sun to stand still and the moon to stop! What an amazing God!

The next story comes from a woman of Canaan whose

53

daughter was possessed by demons, and she refused to be sent away by Jesus and his disciples until she received healing for her daughter:

> *Leaving that place, Jesus withdrew to the region of Tyre and Sidon. A Canaanite woman from that vicinity came to him, crying out, "Lord, Son of David, have mercy on me! My daughter is demon-possessed and suffering terribly." Jesus did not answer a word. So his disciples came to him and urged him, "Send her away, for she keeps crying out after us." He answered, "I was sent only to the lost sheep of Israel." The woman came and knelt before him. "Lord, help me!" she said. He replied, "It is not right to take the children's bread and toss it to the dogs." "Yes it is, Lord," she said. "Even the dogs eat the crumbs that fall from their master's table." Then Jesus said to her, "Woman, you have great faith! Your request is granted." And her daughter was healed at that moment.*
>
> *- Mathew 15:21-28(NIV)*

The woman of Canaan did not let offense stop her from obtaining her goal - healing for her daughter. She didn't let the comments of Jesus or even his disciples impede her progress and because of her persistence, she received what she came for – healing for her daughter. [25]

Similarly, because of our persistence, we received the transfer for Jordanne to attend the highly ranked secondary school for girls. We didn't allow the situation to cause us any embarrassment. We stood in faith for one outcome to the point where we didn't consider any alternatives. Almighty God was on our side, nudging us on to victory!

WATCH OUT FOR UNBELIEF!

You can move mountains even if your faith is as tiny as a mustard seed. Only unbelief will stop you from doing the impossible. Even Jesus didn't do miracles in certain places because of the environment of unbelief.

> *Jesus went out from there and came into His hometown; and His disciples followed Him. When the Sabbath came, He began to teach in the synagogue; and the many listeners were astonished, saying, "Where did this man get these things, and what is this wisdom given to Him, and such miracles as these performed by His hands? "Is not this the carpenter, the son of Mary, and brother of James and Joses and Judas and Simon? Are not His sisters here with us?" And*

they took offense at Him. Jesus said to them, "A prophet is not without honor except in his hometown and among his own relatives and in his own household." And He could do no miracle there except that He laid His hands on a few sick people and healed them. And He wondered at their unbelief.

-Mark 6:1-6 (NAS)

Sometimes, it is not only unbelief but doubt that causes a faith failure (Luke 17:5-6, Mark 11:23, Matthew 21:21, Matthew 17:20). [26]

Faith and unbelief both come by hearing and what we focus our thoughts on every day. We can choose to feed our faith or feed our unbelief and doubt by the things we read, the music we listen to and the voices we allow to speak to us. I pray you will choose to feed your faith which comes by hearing the Word of God (Romans 10:17, Mark 4:24), then you will see the impossible made possible through Jesus Christ.

If there are any areas of unbelief and doubt in your life, increasing your time in the Word of God and prayer will help improve the quality of your faith. Today, I encourage you to feed your faith and starve your unbelief to death! May the Lord continue to bless and keep you always!

CHAPTER SEVEN

FORSAKING OTHERS MAY BE NECESSARY

"Many Christians want the benefits of their belief, but they hesitate at the cost of discipleship."[27]
— Billy Graham

WHEN GOD IS TAKING YOU TO A HIGHER HEIGHT, A new position, or a new place, not everyone can go with you. The destiny is yours to fulfill! God has a specific plan and purpose for your life, for which He created you to accomplish. You are unique, a designer's original, and extremely special to God. It is vital for you to recognize, it is your destiny to fulfill and not the destiny of others. It may be logical to think that people who matter to you, like family and friends, should be part of God's plan for your life, but this may not necessarily be the case.

Take the story of Abraham or Abram as an example. When God called Abram out of Haran where he dwelt with his wife Sarai, his nephew Lot, and father Terah, the call was explicit to Abram. After Abram's father died in Haran, Genesis 12: 1-4 tells us:

> *Now the Lord had said unto Abram, Get thee out of thy country, and from thy kindred, and from thy father's house, unto a land that I will shew thee: And I will make of thee a great nation, and I will bless thee, and make thy name great; and thou shalt be a blessing: And I will bless them that bless thee, and curse him that curseth thee: and in thee shall all families of the earth be blessed. So, Abram departed, as the Lord had spoken unto him; and Lot went with him: and Abram was seventy and five years old when he departed out of Haran.*
>
> - Genesis 12:1- 4(KJV)

As the verse reveals, the promise of God's blessing was intended for Abram. It was his destiny to fulfill, yet Lot went with him. Afterward, the relationship between them became strained as explained in the verses below:

And there was strife between the herdsmen of Abram's livestock and the herdsmen of Lot's livestock. Now the Canaanite and the Perizzite were dwelling then in the land. So, Abram said to Lot, "Please let there be no strife between you and me, nor between my herdsmen and your herdsmen, for we are brothers. "Is not the whole land before you? Please separate from me; if to the left, then I will go to the right; or if to the right, then I will go to the left." Lot lifted up his eyes and saw all the valley of the Jordan, that it was well watered everywhere—this was before the LORD destroyed Sodom and Gomorrah—like the garden of the LORD, like the land of Egypt as you go to Zoar. So, Lot chose for himself all the valley of the Jordan, and Lot journeyed eastward. Thus, they separated from each other. Abram settled in the land of Canaan, while Lot settled in the cities of the valley, and moved his tents as far as Sodom

- Genesis 13:7-12 (NAS)

It seemed logical that Abram would take his nephew Lot on the journey with him. In hindsight, I believe Abram could have averted the strife if he had enquired of the Lord whom to take on his journey. It was after the separation that the Lord reiterated His promises to Abram:

The LORD said to Abram, after Lot had sepa-
rated from him, "Now lift up your eyes and look
from the place where you are, northward and
southward and eastward and westward; for all
the land which you see, I will give it to you and to
your descendants forever. "I will make your de-
scendants as the dust of the earth, so that if any-
one can number the dust of the earth, then your
descendants can also be numbered. "Arise, walk
about the land through its length and breadth;
for I will give it to you." Then Abram moved his
tent and came and dwelt by the oaks of Mamre,
which are in Hebron, and there he built an altar
to the LORD.

- *Genesis 13:14-18(NAS)*

As the story progresses, we are told that God rescued Lot and his family from their dwelling place in Sodom and Gomorrah before its destruction. "Would Lot and his family require rescuing if Abram had asked God who should go with him?"

Thus, the message here is to ask the Lord who should help accomplish your purpose. Not everyone is part of the destiny God has planned for you, and you may insist on taking along others to their own peril.

ALWAYS ENQUIRE OF THE LORD

Our experience was again quite like Abram. The Lord called my three children and me out of Jamaica to venture into new territory. As time progressed, I began to encourage my mother to come along with us. She told me that she would pray about the decision. In the interim, she did absolutely nothing! Sometime after, she informed me of her decision to stay in Jamaica. It was quite a devastating blow, but I was determined to follow God's direction for our lives.

While trying to overcome the disappointment of my mother's decision, I was harboring another kind of heartache. Briana, my second child, was not elated about the prospect of leaving Jamaica. I was cognizant that she had worked very hard to get into the top school in Jamaica. Migration was likely to place her at a disadvantage being in lower six-form with one year to go before university. Moreover, she was the only one who had maintained her current group of friends throughout her six years of secondary school. I knew migration was going to be a difficult sell to her, and indeed, it was! She wasn't agreeable to our plans, especially not at a time when she had dreams of completing six-form in Jamaica and later attending university either in Jamaica or the USA.

My options were to obey the Lord and follow His path for our lives or stay in Jamaica for the sake of Briana. While

I contemplated my decision, the Lord became very silent. In the deafening silence, I could hear the Scripture, "...*Chose you this day whom you shall serve....*" (Joshua 24:15). I was resolute I was going to follow the direction of the Lord.

I continued to engage Briana about our plans and the importance of obeying the Lord. I prayed continuously for the Lord to work on her heart. Unsurprisingly, most of her friends couldn't fathom why I was taking her out of school with one year left to complete six-form. Even my boss thought our plans were ill-conceived. Unbeknown to them, we were in the final stages of our plans, and preparations were in high gear as the plans were being birthed. The Lord eventually worked on Briana's heart. She accepted our plans halfheartedly and got involved in the preparations.

Fourth Dream

Shortly after, I had another dream. I was in my front lawn, and I noticed that my four massive palm trees had been uprooted, leaving big gaping holes in the ground. I was outraged that someone would have the audacity to come into my front lawn and uproot my palm trees, after so many years of nurturing them.

When I arose from the dream, I prayed about it, and then I went outside and anointed my palm trees with olive oil. Sometime after, I received the revelation from the Holy Spirit. The four palm trees uprooted represented what was about to happen to four of us. The dream was confirmation that our migration plans involved only four of us. My mother was not part of our journey. Thank God for a praying mother who decided to seek the Lord first rather than heed my request to come along with us.

ASKING THE RIGHT QUESTIONS

There is wisdom in asking God the right questions. God is not afraid of your questions, even your unbelief. Just ask God, "Who should be part of my journey?" "How will it happen?" and "How should I prepare?" Trust God to provide the answers.

The story of Abraham underscores the importance of asking the right questions. The Bible tells us that Sarai was barren when the Lord confirmed that a child would come forth from Abram's bowels. Abram had only enquired of the lord what he would give him seeing that he was childless:

> *Since You have given no offspring to me, one born in my house is my heir. Then behold, the*

word of the LORD came to him, saying, "This man
will not be your heir; but one who will come forth
from your own body, he shall be your heir."
- Genesis 15:3-4(NAS)

God's response to Abram presented him with the opportunity to ask God, "how would this be seeing that Sarai and I are old, and Sarai is barren?" Mary, the mother of Jesus, was in a similar situation. The angel of the Lord visited her and told her she would become pregnant, and she asked, "how can this be since I am a virgin?" and the answer was given to her in Luke 1:35, when the angel answered and said to her, "The Holy Spirit will come upon you, and the power of the Most High will overshadow you; and for that reason the holy Child shall be called the Son of God." Abram did not ask God the pertinent question. In the following chapter, we learn of Sarai's attempt to bring forth the heir in her strength:

> *Now Sarai Abram's wife bare him no children:*
> *and she had a handmaid, an Egyptian, whose*
> *name was Hagar. And Sarai said unto Abram, be-*
> *hold now, the Lord hath restrained me from*
> *bearing: I pray thee, go in unto my maid; it may*
> *be that I may obtain children by her. And Abram*
> *hearkened to the voice of Sarai.*
- Genesis 16:1-2 (KJV)

The Bible tells us that after Hagar bore the son Ishmael, strife developed between her and Sarai and Sarai sent her away. Sometime afterward, Sarai bore a son, called Isaac at the age of ninety years.

Today, the war continues between Israel (the seed of Isaac) and Iran and Iraq, (the seed of Ishmael) both children of Abram. "Could this generational curse have been averted if Abram and Sarah had asked of the Lord who the promise of Abram's heir was to come from?" The lesson is to ask the Lord the pertinent questions.

LEAVING OTHERS BEHIND IS PAINFUL

It is so important to seek God's guidance and ask the relevant questions to accomplish God's plan for your life. At times, the response from God may require you to forsake others – mother, father, husband, wives, brother, sister and friends to follow Jesus and the unique path He has for you. Leaving other behind does not mean that you must cut them off, but whatever the Lord has planned for you, not everyone can go with you. Some must remain to cheer you on, while others, may not be part of your destiny.

Jesus had to forsake others during His earthly mission. He came on this earth to fulfill His Father's will; His destiny - The Cross; His purpose – the salvation of humanity (Philippian 2:8). At an early age, Jesus parted from His parents to stay behind in the Church to do His Father's business (Luke 2:41-49). He later began His mission with seventy-two disciples. However, not all could stand His teachings, and they departed leaving twelve, one betrayer and eleven others who couldn't go to the cross with Him. It was His calling, His destiny, His Father's will and only He alone could accomplish it. In Luke 14 Jesus says:

> *If anyone comes to me and does not hate his own father and mother and wife and children and brothers and sisters, yes, and even his own life, he cannot be my disciple. Whoever does not carry his own cross and come after me cannot be my disciple. So likewise, whoever of you does not forsake all that he has cannot be my disciple.*
>
> *- Luke 14:26-27 (KJV)*

This verse means if you want to follow Jesus and His will for your life, you must be willing to leave or forsake the people in your life whom you have previously loved the most...parents, spouses, children and siblings. When should someone do this? If these people are not willing to follow Jesus or are not a part of God's destiny for your life, then they must be forsaken.

Jesus is merely teaching one of the implications of the greatest command, which is to love the Lord your God with all your heart, soul, mind and strength (Mathew 22:37). If we do this, by listening to God and following His commands, other people formerly close in our lives may accuse us of hating them because we no longer listen to their advice first in how we live our lives.

Jesus adds that we must even hate our own life in this world if we are to follow Him and gain eternal life. Those who seek to keep their lives in this world will lose eternal life with Him (Luke 17:33). It is the most profound and purest meaning of Jesus' command that we "forsake all." He emphasizes forsaking all - our own lives and all the closest natural relationships to make sure we get the point.

It is indeed hard teaching for most of us, but don't lose heart the rewards are far greater as Jesus tells Peter in Mathew 19:27-30:

> *Then answered Peter and said unto him, Behold, we have forsaken all, and followed thee; what shall we have therefore? And Jesus said unto them, Verily I say unto you, that ye which have followed me, in the regeneration when the Son of man shall sit in the throne of his glory, ye also shall sit upon twelve thrones, judging the twelve tribes of Israel. And everyone that hath forsaken houses, or brethren, or sisters, or father, or mother, or wife, or children, or lands, for my name's sake, shall receive an hundredfold, and*

shall inherit everlasting life. But many that are
first shall be last; and the last shall be first.

\- Matthew 19:27-30 (KJV)

I have lost many friends since I made a personal commitment to follow Jesus. Many thought my new-found faith was a phase, and I would soon snap out of it, but it's been over fourteen years now. I have drawn even closer to God, and when the time was right, God brought the right people into my life.

Leaving others behind might be necessary to follow God's direction for your life, but it is a tough call. I think the most painful experience for us was leaving my mother, other family members and friends in Jamaica to follow God's plan for our lives. As painful as it was, especially to leave my mother behind, I realized God's plan was for my children and me and not for her. It was our purpose to accomplish.

My prayer for you as you ponder on the next phase, next dream or next journey that you seek the Lord, ask the right questions and wait on Him for the answers.

CHAPTER EIGHT

FAITH STANDS IN THE POWER OF GOD

"Don't tell me how big your mountain is. Tell
your mountain how BIG your God is."[28]
– Benson Idahosa

WHEN I HAD THOSE INITIAL DREAMS, MY response was to heed the plans of God for our lives. I told my friend, Patricia about my dreams and no one else, as I perceived people might think I was foolish. As our plans progressed, I was able to speak more freely to other people about my dreams and the direction of God's plan.

Olivia and I had already received offers from a university in London and Manchester. It was shortly afterward that I had another dream.

Fifth Dream

In this dream, I was getting ready to fly to a destination, but I was running late. I saw myself frantically throwing clothes into a suitcase and hurriedly packing to catch the flight. I arose from the dream, knowing I had to expedite our arrangements.

Shortly after, I advertised our house for sale and received an offer within two weeks. Since the third dream showed me an empty house, I began selling the contents of our home. We sold most of it within three months.

We did all we could in the natural and awaited God's supernatural power to open the right doors to aid us financially. Obtaining adequate funding was a big part of the plan. We didn't have enough funds! I wasn't quite sure what route to take when it came to obtaining funding for School. When my boss mentioned study-leave, I felt it was a good idea at the time. I surmised that if this isn't in keeping with God's plan, the Lord will close the door.

I mentioned the study-leave to the head of the area, and he wasn't very receptive of the idea. I left his office thinking, either way, God was going to work it out. I submitted my study-leave application and awaited the decision. I had a feeling this wasn't the route, considering the study-leave policy required employees to return to the company on completion of their program of study or repay the bond.

I was in my office with a longtime friend, Judith, who was visiting from the UK, when someone called to relay the outcome of my study-leave application. The decision was "no!" Judith was very disturbed and enquired about my next move. Instantly I knew the answer – resignation! I penned my resignation letter immediately to ensure I served the required notice period. I received help from Patricia who had been privy to all our plans. Judith was shocked! She asked me if I was sure about what I was doing and, "Why are you throwing away fifteen years of service like that?" "where are the funds for schooling going to come from?" and "how are you going to survive with three children, in a strange country with no job?"

My boss was also perplexed. Surely, she thought that with no study-leave granted, I would have changed my mind, as she felt my plans were too hasty. Can you imagine if I had replied saying I was being led by dreams from God? They probably would think I was crazy. God's plan for our lives didn't follow conventional wisdom. Therefore, my response was to assure them that all will be well.

I had some savings. I surmised that from the sale of our house I could fund our education. However, I knew it wasn't enough. I continued to pray about it and pressed on with our plans. By this time, the church, my co-workers and our friends and family became aware of our plans, and they supported by purchasing the contents of our home.

Sixth Dream

By end July (one month before leaving Jamaica), I had another dream from God. This time I saw myself pregnant, walking on a street that didn't look familiar. I was in the road, having just emerged from among parked cars. I took note that the vehicles were small and parked in a row on the street. Suddenly, a lady appeared from nowhere and asked if I needed a ride. She told me we could take one of the cars parked on the road. I reluctantly agreed but asked her if taking the car would not be considered stealing. She replied that this was not Jamaica and taking the car was fine as long as she contacted the owner and returned the vehicle. I went with her, and she dropped me off at a building resembling a university building. I saw myself in a huge classroom with only a handful of students. When the class was over, I considered how I was going to get home. I went outside, and lo, the lady appeared again from nowhere, asking if I needed a ride back home. I asked her what she did with the car, and she told me the owner came for the vehicle. She gave me a lift back home.

I arose from the dream with the confirmation that I was going to the UK. I didn't receive any revelation from God concerning the person who gave me the ride. However, I knew I was pregnant with a mission, a plan or an idea to be birthed in the UK while attending school. I prayed, knowing God will make all things possible by His supernatural power.

THE INFALLIBLE POWER OF GOD

The only way you can accomplish those dreams, goals, and missions God has placed in your heart is through His supernatural power. God's supernatural power accomplished every major transformational feat undertaken by people in the Bible. Our faith in Him unleashes His supernatural power. The parting of the Red Sea (Exodus 14:21) was accomplished only through the obedience of Moses to God's calling to rescue the Israelites from Egypt. I Corinthians 2 says:

> *That your faith should not stand in the wisdom of men but in the power of God.*
> - 1 Corinthians 2:5 (KJV)

Who knows the extent of the power of God? Who can fathom His might and power? No one! All that we know is that God is all-powerful and exceedingly mighty. He is omnipotent, omniscient and omnipresent. "For my thoughts are not your thoughts, neither are your ways my ways," saith the Lord, "For as the heavens are higher than the earth, so are my ways higher than your ways, and my thoughts than your thoughts" (Isaiah 55: 8–9).

God spoke the universe into existence; a universe that astronomers estimate contains more than 100 billion galaxies. Moreover, all the power contained in the entire universe is but a small representation of the unlimited power of God. The combined energy of all earth's storms, winds, and other forces of nature do not equal even a fraction of God's Almighty power. God's power is inherent in His nature. All power is His and will continue to be His for all eternity.[29] Ephesians 1:17 states:

> *That the God of our Lord Jesus Christ, the Father of glory, may give to you a spirit of wisdom and of revelation in the knowledge of Him. I pray that the eyes of your heart may be enlightened, so that you will know what is the hope of His calling, what are the riches of the glory of His inheritance in the saints; and what is the surpassing greatness of His power toward us who believe. These are in accordance with the working of the strength of His might; which He brought about in Christ, when He raised Him from the dead and seated Him at His right hand in the heavenly places; far above all rule and authority and power and dominion, and every name that is*

named, not only in this age but also in the one to come.

- Ephesians1:17-21 (NAS)

God operates outside the box, and no one can comprehend His mighty power. There are tremendous accomplishments and miracles wrought by the power of God that didn't follow conventional wisdom. For example, turning water into wine was accomplished because of obedience (St. John 2:1-11) and the sun standing still so Joshua could continue fighting (Joshua 10:12-14).

Any power that we have is given to us by God. Because God is all-powerful, He has the ability and strength to do whatever He pleases. His power is not restrained or inhibited by any of His created beings. People and nations are powerless when confronted by His Might. This fantastic God can do anything as long as it does not violate any of His other attributes.[30] No task is too big for Him. Jeremiah 32:27 says, "Behold, I am the Lord, the God of all flesh. Is there anything too hard for Me?" God never fails, and He is never tired or discouraged (Psalm 121:1-8). Our all-powerful Creator cares for us, and He longs to exhibit His power in our lives. David, the writer of the Psalms, puts it this way:

When I look at the night sky and see the work of Your fingers, the moon and the stars You have set

> *in place-what are mortals that You should think*
> *of us, mere humans that You should care for us?*
> - Psalm 8:3, 4(NIV)

When you know God is Almighty, this will give you un-shakeable confidence in Him. It is the same confidence Abraham displayed when God told him to sacrifice his son (Hebrews 11:17-19). He reckoned that God could raise him from the dead. It was the same confidence Jesus had when he suffered the cross and endured the shame for the salvation of the world. Jesus knew that God would raise Him on the third day! (1 Corinthians 15:4). This level of confidence is predicated on knowing that God is Almighty, mighty to save, mighty to deliver, and there is nothing, that is too hard for Him to do! [31]

No matter what you might be facing today, God can help you. No need is too great for Him to meet. No problem is too complicated for Him to solve. No foe is too strong for Him to conquer. No prayer is too difficult for Him to answer. The Bible promises that "By His mighty power at work within us, He can accomplish infinitely more than we could ever dare to ask or hope" (Ephesians 3:20). If our hearts and motives are pure and we genuinely seek to do God's will, then there is nothing too difficult for us as we depend on His strength.[32] Therefore, let your faith stand in the power of God and not in the wisdom of men!

THE FALLIBLE WISDOM OF MEN

Too often people rely on the wisdom of men and not on the power of God. They put their faith in people to open doors for them, to get that new job or new contract. People might sometimes use the phrase, 'I am well connected.' Does this sound familiar? My response has always been, 'To who are you well connected?' God's advice on this matter is clear:

> *Do not trust in princes, in mortal man, in whom there is no salvation. His spirit departs, he returns to the earth; In that very day his thoughts perish. How blessed is he whose help is the God of Jacob; Whose hope is in the LORD his God.*
> - Psalm 146:3-5 (NAS)

What is the wisdom of man in comparison to the knowledge of the all-knowing and only wise God? What is man, who doesn't know what will happen tomorrow, who is here today, gone tomorrow? (James 4:14). What is the wisdom of man? The Bible says:

> *For since in the wisdom of God the world through its wisdom did not come to know God, God was well-pleased through the foolishness of the message preached to save those who believe. For indeed Jews ask for signs and Greeks search for*

wisdom; but we preach Christ crucified, to Jews a stumbling block and to Gentiles foolishness, but to those who are the called, both Jews and Greeks, Christ the power of God and the wisdom of God. Because the foolishness of God is wiser than men, and the weakness of God is stronger than men.

- 1 Corinthians 1:21-25 (NAS)

If you depend on the wisdom of men at the expense of seeking God's wisdom, you will never accomplish great feats for God. Men are ever learning and coming up with new ideas and theories. Some choose whatever ideals, morals, and 'truths' works best for that day and age, and others when it suits their agenda, deny the very existence of an Almighty God. The Bible says that, "the invisible things of God from the creation of the world are clearly seen; being understood by the things that are made, even His eternal power and Godhead; so that men are without excuse."

But God has chosen the foolish things of the world to shame the wise, and God has chosen the weak things of the world to shame the things which are strong; and the base things of the world and the despised. God has chosen the things that are not; so that He may nullify the things that are, so that no man may boast before God.

- 1 Corinthians 1:27-29 (NAS)

The wisdom of men is fallible! They will tell you believing God is nonsense; the Bible is out of sync with the times, and what God is asking you to do is ludicrous. Don't let anyone talk you out of believing God or discourage you from pursuing His purpose for your life. You can't prove anything through man's wisdom; they don't know what the future holds. I urge you to believe in God as your foundation of truth. For us, it is thus saith the LORD!

WALK IN THE COUNSEL OF THE GODLY

One month before leaving Jamaica, I had sold most of the contents of our home. I sold my old car, and I received an offer on the house. We purchased one-way tickets to the UK, but the question remained about the unsold items in our house.

I was sitting in my office haggling over the price of my sofa with a coworker who wanted to purchase the item for pennies. She cheekily mentioned that since I wasn't willing to reduce the price, I should ship my stuff. Immediately, I asked the Lord about shipping the remainder of our stuff, and I had peace about the decision. I also spoke to Patricia, and she thought it was an excellent idea. I shipped the rest of our stuff, including work attire which I tried desperately to sell but couldn't sell.

Again, we just kept listening to God and following His plan for our lives. I was careful to listen to advice from Godly people. Opinions of others who thought, it was the wrong time, we didn't know what we were doing; it would be difficult to survive in a new country with three children without a job didn't persuade us. We knew that obeying God's plan for our lives always unleashes His provision, protection, and divine favor! Hence our faith didn't stand in the wisdom of men but in the Mighty power of God!

I pray today that you allow your faith to stand in the power of God and not in the wisdom of men. Be assured that obeying God always leads to miraculous and astounding results! May your decision today redound to God's honor and glory!

CHAPTER NINE

FIGHT THE GOOD FIGHT OF FAITH

*"I have been driven many times upon my knees
by the overwhelming conviction that I had nowhere else to go. My own wisdom and that of all
about me seemed insufficient for that day."*[33]
— *Abraham Lincoln*

YES, THERE WILL BE CHALLENGES TO YOUR FAITH!
There will be times when you will be tempted to give up and quit. However, I encourage you to keep fighting and running your race! Your dreams, your goals or the desires God has placed within you is just around the corner. Don't quit while you are ahead! A great reward will await you at the finish line! The Bible puts it this way:

Fight the good fight of faith; take hold of the eternal life to which you were called, and you made the good confession in the presence of many witnesses.

- 1Timothy 6:12 (NAS)

OUR FIGHT OF FAITH!

No matter what happens, fight the good fight of faith! For us, it was a constant battle which intensified when we got to the airport to board our flight to the UK. Now that the dreams were coming into fruition, all hell broke loose!

Before leaving Jamaica, we tried to plan for housing in the UK. We enlisted the help of a family member in London to contact friends in Manchester who could help us find accommodation. I also searched earnestly for rental properties. However, the issue was trying to negotiate with agents to rent properties without being present to view them. Our family member enlisted the help of her friend in Manchester to view suitable rental properties for us. Eventually, she became tired and decided she could no longer assist us in viewing properties, but she provided a contact, who had a property we could rent as a last resort. I contacted this friend and was told that on arrival at the Manchester airport we should contact her to view the house. If suitable, we could pay on the spot and move in immediately. I asked her to send pictures of the property in advance, and she indicated she couldn't send the pictures. I had a premonition of imminent disaster about this arrangement. I continued to pray to the Lord for the right accommodation.

We arrived at Manchester airport in early September, cleared our luggage and were now awaiting further instructions from the property owners. After several calls and no response, I asked my family to book us into a hotel until we heard from the owners of the property. Eventually, we did! We took a taxi from the airport and went to see the property with the intention of renting immediately. When we arrived and went inside the house, the place was unbelievable - it was a dump! We left so quickly, headed straight to the hotel and checked in for four nights until we could find suitable accommodation.

On the fourth day, I checked out of the hotel because it was costly to maintain two hotel rooms between four of us. I called a taxi, and we tried almost every hotel in the area until we found a reasonably priced hotel. We checked in for another four nights. The hotel was comfortable, and it gave us the chance to regroup and seek God's direction. My prayer life became very intense during that period, and I constantly reminded God that He brought us here and we were dependent on Him solely to see us through.

I was aware that Briana and Jordanne should have been enrolled in school already. Armed with the two choices for school we selected while in Jamaica, we got up and set out on our journey. We visited the school closest to the hotel first to get Briana into six-form and Jordanne into grade eight. When the head of learning for the six-form school saw Briana's exceptional grades, she was offered a place on the spot to begin school the next day. The only issue was that Briana had to re-sit lower six-form given the difference in the A 'level exam structure in the UK. We were aware that this might happen, but Briana was very miserable about the situation.

The school informed me that I would need to write to the Council for Jordanne to be accepted in the same school. Nevertheless, Briana started attending school from the hotel. I wrote to the Council and the school telling them why I required both my children to attend the same school. I prayed continuously and waited on God to open those doors. In the meantime, I kept calling the school to enquire on the progress.

I was scheduled to check out of the hotel on the fourth day. On day two, I was still searching for rental properties. Most rental agencies have extensive verification processes, but I didn't engage with them based on the urgency of our situation. I located other rental properties, but the owners either refused to accept upfront payments or wanted to engage in a bidding war. At the end of day two, I went to renew my stay at the hotel, only to be told the hotel was fully booked for the next three days. What a calamity! No house in hand and no hotel to stay in and all surrounding hotels were fully booked because of the football match, involving Manchester United.

On day four, I arose early armed with three rental properties to view. We checked out of the hotel, and my girls stayed in the hotel lobby while I proceeded to see these properties. I ruled out the first and second property based on the lengthy turnaround time. I continued to cry out to God for help in finding a house that night, not the next day, but that night! Being homeless was not an option! The last property on my list was in Old Trafford, Manchester. It was furnished, and it seemed ideal. I negotiated the price and told the agent I needed the place that night. I got the place, paid upfront for six months and moved in at 11:00 pm that night. God came through again in the nick of time!

The options were to fight or risk becoming homeless. Fight I did! I fought the battle in prayer, reminding God of His promises and our obedience. I also fought the battle by being persistent and not quitting. God responded mightily, every time our circumstances became unbearable. He is indeed an ever-present help in times of trouble (Psalm 46:1). I give Him all the glory and the praise! Hallelujah to His Mighty Name!

Put On Your Gloves And Fight!

In this world, you will face many circumstances that may cause you to falter in your faith, such as the state of the economy, impending wars, daily life, and family issues. However, it is during these moments that you must fight the good fight of faith!

You know from the Word of God, that He will supply all your needs according to His riches in glory (Philippians 4:19); you know He will never leave nor forsake you (Hebrews 13:5) and you know He said that whatever you ask for in prayer, believing and you shall receive (Mark 11:24). Don't start doubting His Word because circumstances appear contrary to what you expected.

When circumstances get tough, and everything looks dark and hopeless, lay hold on the promises of God and operate in faith and not by sight. Believe in God and trust in His Word no matter what - God will cause you to be victorious if you don't quit. Stay in the fight of faith! Make up your mind to win! [34]

Many mighty acts were wrought by men and women who refused to give up their faith in God. They kept their faith in God stalwart and strong in the face of every obstacle they encountered in life! If they could do it, so can you. God is the same God now as He was then! What He did for those who trusted Him in the past, He'll do for you today![35] As Hebrews 11:32 conveys;

> *And what shall I more say? for the time would*
> *fail me to tell of Gideon, and of Barak, and of*
> *Samson, and of Jephthae; of David also, and Sam-*
> *uel, and of the prophets: Who through faith sub-*
> *dued kingdoms, wrought righteousness, ob-*
> *tained promises, stopped the mouths of lions;*
> *Quenched the violence of fire, escaped the edge*
> *of the sword, out of weakness were made strong,*
> *waxed valiant in fight, turned to flight the armies*
> *of the aliens.*
>
> -Hebrews 11:32–34 (KJV)

The people God used were those who refused to quit! They weren't people who were necessarily any braver, wiser, or smarter than you are. They were just people with tenacity and determination of faith who wouldn't take "no" for an answer!

Today, there are many Christians who are taking "no" for an answer or believing the enemy's lies especially when victory is around the corner. The enemy is a liar, telling people they won't achieve their dreams, they won't get well, they will always struggle with their finances, and they will forever remain poor. These are all lies! Yet people believe the lie, and back away from the victory around the corner, instead of pressing ahead in faith.[36] God has promised you an abundant life. His Word says, "The thief comes only to steal and kill and destroy; I came that they may have life and have it abundantly" (John 10:10). Claim the abundant life Jesus offers you. God's supply is not limited, in short supply or running out! Have a mentality that refuses to quit. Be determined to follow God's plan for your life and don't turn aside from following Jesus no matter what! If you stay faithful to God's Word, you are assured the victory in every circumstance.[37]

WITNESSES WATCHING AND CHEERING YOU ON

A great cloud of witnesses is watching and cheering you on, providing you with another reason why you should never quit fighting the good fight of faith. My children were watching to see how I managed both favorable and unfavorable circumstances. Friends and family were watching to see how we were going to survive. Others watched to see if the God we professed to serve would come through for us. The Bible says:

> *Wherefore seeing we also are compassed about with so great a cloud of witnesses, let us lay aside every weight, and the sin which doth so easily beset us, and let us run with patience the race that is set before us. Looking unto Jesus the author and finisher of our faith; who for the joy that was set before him endured the cross, despising the*

shame, and is set down at the right hand of the
throne of God.

- Hebrews 12:1-2 (KJV)

In this scripture, the writer, Paul uses the image of the ancient Greek games—as an illustration for the verse above. In ancient Greece, the athletes prepared for the Greek games by wearing heavyweights on their legs and arms and armor-like plates on their bodies as they trained. The training was undertaken for endurance and strength before the actual contest.[38]

In the actual games, however, those athletes laid aside the heavyweights, making their bodies weightless and movements effortless with a significant increase in endurance and stamina. The stands were full of cheering spectators who watched the athletes as they ran their races and competed with great strength and endurance.[39]

Paul uses this imagery of the Greek games like a picture of the Christian running the race of life, pressing on to the finish line. Compassed around with a great cloud of witnesses just as the Greek athletes were surrounded by spectators cheering them on from the stands.

My friend be assured that many people are cheering you on as you run your race. The whole host of the heavenly family, our loved ones and even strangers are all watching from the grandstand, cheering you on to victory.[40] More witnesses are for you than they are against you. The story of Elisha in the Bible confirms this truth:

> *Now when the attendant of the man of God had risen early and gone out, behold, an army with horses and chariots was circling the city. And his servant said to him, "Alas, my master! What shall we do?" So, he answered "Do not fear, for those who are with us are more than those who are with them." Then Elisha prayed and said, "O LORD, I pray, open his eyes that he may see." And the LORD opened the servant's eyes and he saw; and behold, the mountain was full of horses and chariots of fire all around Elisha.*
> - 2 Kings 6:15-17 (NAS)

The Word also reminds you that you are more than a conqueror through Jesus who gives you strength (Romans 8:37-39). Today, I encourage you to get up, stand tall and be counted! Regardless of what your situation looks like, don't give up on your purpose or goals, destiny is calling you! Therefore, Fight the good fight of faith, run your race with patience and confidence, and more importantly, cross the finish line! A great cloud of witnesses is watching from the stand and cheering you on to victory. Don't give up on

God's promises to you! Fight the good fight of faith to the very end! You shall receive the reward from God.

STAND FIRMLY ANCHORED IN GOD'S WORD

While it is essential to fight and don't give up on the life God has set for you, it is also critical that you don't lose sight of the bigger goal which is eternal life with Jesus. Fighting the good fight of faith is, therefore, fighting to the very end of your life to guarantee eternal life with Jesus. This is the ultimate goal! Don't ever lose sight of this goal while you run your race on earth.

Those who want to be faithful to God know that living an overcomer's life in the virtues of Christ is not something that comes automatically. Fighting the good fight of faith means that we stand firmly anchored in the Word of God, in the power of the Holy Spirit, reckoning ourselves dead to our feelings and our human reasoning and not letting sin rule in our mortal body.[41]

The Bible speaks of a narrow way - the cross, self-denial and holy and righteous living. The Bible is full of serious exhortations. Words such as, "Work out your own salvation with fear and trembling ..." (Philippians 2:12). "Strive to enter through the narrow gate ..." (Luke 13:24). "Take heed to yourself and to the doctrine. Continue in them ..." (1 Timothy 4:16). "Exercise yourself rather to godliness." (1 Timothy 4:7). "But also, for this very reason, giving all diligence, add to your faith virtue ..." (2 Peter 1:5). "Therefore, brethren, be even more diligent to make your calling and election sure ..." (2 Peter 1:10).[42]

Jesus sent the Holy Spirit precisely to give us the power to fight the good fight of faith to the very end. Let us choose to hear the Word of God and follow His commands as enumerated in I Timothy 6:11-14

> *But flee from these things, you man of God, and pursue righteousness, godliness, faith, love, perseverance and gentleness. Fight the good fight of faith; take hold of the eternal life to which you were called, and you made the good confession in the presence of many witnesses. I charge you in the presence of God, who gives life to all things, and of Christ Jesus, who testified the good confession before Pontius Pilate; that you keep the commandment without stain or reproach until the appearing of our Lord Jesus Christ,*
>
> - 1 Timothy 6:11-14 (NAS)

Whatever your situation is today, don't give up on God! Don't give up on life! Fight the good fight of faith! Lay hold on His promises, and He will surely make you victorious!

CHAPTER TEN

Taking Up Your Cross Daily

"If you have not experienced the death of self,
your spiritual life will have little real pro-
gress."[43]
– Watchman Nee

TAKING UP YOUR CROSS DAILY REQUIRES A lifelong commitment to walking by faith. This faith dimension is a whole new ballgame; in a league all by itself. I pondered hard before writing this chapter, as I perceived this was going to be the hardest teaching. Taking up your cross is symbolic of following Jesus daily. Whatever the season, day or challenge, God expects you to take up your cross daily and follow Him:

And he said to them all, if any man will come af-
ter me, let him deny himself, and take up his cross
daily, and follow me. For whosoever will save his
life shall lose it: but whosoever will lose his life
for my sake, the same shall save it. For what is a
man advantaged, if he gains the whole world,
and lose himself, or be cast away?

- Luke 9:23–25 (KJV)

The first verse says if anyone wants to follow Jesus, he or she must do two things. They must "deny themselves" and "take up their cross daily."

To deny oneself means to say "No" to self and "Yes" to God. It is to submit your will to God daily. It is to go through life repeating the words that Jesus said the night before He died while praying to God in the garden of Gethsemane. He said, "Not my will but yours be done" (Luke 22:42). It is what millions of Christians have prayed for centuries when they repeat the "Lord's Prayer," "Your will be done, on earth as it is in heaven" (Matthew 6:10).[44]

To come to Jesus Christ for salvation is to come to the end of self and sin and to seek His righteousness. "Seek ye first the kingdom of God and His righteousness, and all these things shall be added unto you" (Matthew 6:33). "Death to self" does not mean asceticism - forgoing earthly possessions, not eating certain foods or ignoring the world. Rather, it signifies "trusting Jesus instead of yourself," and living each day out of an active relationship with God. It means, not falling back to the inferior ways of sin but standing firm in the liberty of Christ.[45]

To "take up his cross daily," indicates a willingness to surrender all to follow Jesus daily. It is called "dying to self" - a call to absolute surrender. Each day, God expects you to surrender to His will and carry your cross of love, joy, forgiveness, mercy, righteousness, holiness, longsuffering, and self-control and follow Him (Galatians 5:22-23).

Before Jesus's death on the cross, the cross was symbolic of pain, shame, and death. A person hung on it, naked until his skeletal structure collapsed, and he suffocated to death, without air and with his body drowning itself in its fluids. When Jesus carried His cross to Golgotha to be crucified, no one thought of the cross as symbolic of a burden to bear. During the time of His crucifixion, the cross meant death by the most torturous, painful and humiliating method. Because the Romans forced convicted criminals to carry their cross to the place of crucifixion, bearing a cross meant carrying their execution device while facing ridicule along the way. However, when Jesus rose triumphantly on the third day, and the disciples proclaimed the good news, the cross then became a cherished symbol of atonement, forgiveness, grace, mercy, and love.[46]

Because of the cross, Christians are expected to live each day in such a way that it is apparent to everyone that we have died to ourselves, our selfish ways and ambitions, and that we now live for God. Another translation says: "If any of you wants to be my follower, you must turn from your selfish ways, take up your cross, and follow me" (NLT). [47]

LIVING DAILY FOR JESUS

There is no other relationship that I value more than my relationship with Jesus Christ. I am continuously in conversation with Him about everything. He is a friend that sticks closer than a brother. I have proven Him as my provider, protector, healer, and Savior. He is my ever-present help in times of trouble. I desire to please God and live a life of holiness and righteousness.

Over the years, the Lord has taught me to recognize His voice. My attitude has always been one of instant obedience to Him. I don't always get it right, but I ask for His forgiveness when I do falter. As much as I love to converse with the Lord in prayer, I also enjoy spending time in His Word, soaking up His wisdom for everyday living.

When we moved to our rental property in Old Trafford, it afforded us the opportunity to settle down for a few months and explore Manchester. Jordanne was still at home awaiting the response from the council and the school regarding her admission. I kept praying earnestly for the Lord to expedite the process so Jordanne could begin school. Sometime after, I received a call from the school requesting Jordanne to come in for a test to determine her class placement. Jordanne took the test and was accepted. I purchased her blazer and some other school attire, but as a goodwill gesture, the school reimbursed the amount I spent on the blazer and tie. I was so grateful and thanked God for His divine favor!

Both Briana and Jordanne were now attending the same school, and Olivia was off to university in London. I was paying international fees for Olivia, and these fees were quite high. While awaiting the sale of our house to pay for Olivia's school fees, my estate agent notified me that the offer fell through because the purchasers couldn't secure a mortgage. I was devastated! But I continued to trust God and prayed for a job. I recognized I had to defer my studies until my family was adequately settled in Manchester and our house sold.

By mid-October, I started applying for jobs in risk management, through recruiters, but some recommended me for jobs I didn't find suitable. Although I had some financial challenges, I knew God would supply all my needs according to His riches in glory. I wasn't prepared to settle for second best. As a result, I turned down some job interviews and continued to apply for suitable jobs while I waited on the Lord. By end November, I received another offer on our house in Jamaica, but by this time my funds had dwindled to a bare minimum.

I continued to seek the Lord persistently in prayer. The best part of this period was the opportunity it gave me to draw closer to the Lord. I was home alone during the days, and I spent time reading my Bible, writing songs to God and downloading ideas from Him about this book. Time at home gave me the chance to help my children adapt to the new environment as well as gain much-needed rest. I learned so many things about God and myself that being in the comfort of my past environment couldn't have taught me. More importantly, I proved God can make a way, where there seems to be no way!

There was a church nearby that we decided to explore one Sunday. We visited the church, and after a few minutes of listening to the service, we discovered that the congregation was mostly Caribbean people, with the Pastor being a Jamaican. It felt like coming home! It felt as if God had transported us back to Jamaica. Wow! God at work again in our lives! We were so elated to have found this church which was within walking distance from our rental home. We attended church and Bible study regularly, which gave us the opportunity to get to know the church, the Pastor and the congregation.

In the meantime, I was still actively looking for a job. I was down to a few hundred pounds, and I heard the Holy Spirit say that I should sow a special financial seed. It would not be the first time I sowed a special seed. The Bible says that we should, "Bring the whole tithe into the storehouse, so that there may be food in My house, and test Me now in this," says the LORD of hosts, "if I will not open for you the windows of heaven and pour out for you a blessing until it overflows. Then I will rebuke the devourer for you, so that it will not destroy the fruits of the ground; nor will your vine in the field cast its grapes, says the LORD of host" (Malachi 3:10).

As I mentioned before, I always endeavor to obey God quickly. I asked the Lord about the amount to sow, and I heard three hundred pounds. Bearing in mind, I only had four hundred pounds in my bank account and didn't know where the funds would come from to survive the Christmas. But I heard the Lord ask me to sow the special seed. It was not easy letting go of the money, but I knew all belonged to Him and He could provide better than I could ever imagine by holding onto the funds. In any event, the money in the Bank couldn't exponentially increase to meet my needs. Only God can supply all my needs according to His riches in glory (Philippians 4:19).

My response was to trust God. I sowed the seed to the church. That week, I received a call from a company that I never applied to for a job. I undertook a phone interview, two face-to-face interviews and was offered the job in December to begin work the first week in January. Oh! Praises to God! God responded to my sacrificial sowing. Glory be to God who continues to provide for us!

I began work in January. On my journey to work that first morning, I was singing and praising God. The Holy Spirit spoke to me about the people I was going to meet and reminded me to love them unconditionally. I received the same message every day for the first week. I continued to heed the voice of God and to love unconditionally. The company was very kind, opting to pay half my salary after two weeks of working there. I was able to pay for Olivia's university fees which became due that month.

Despite the trials and challenges, God's divine favor and presence were always with us. Everything was now beginning to settle down after four months of being in the UK. God provided rental accommodation; the girls were at one of the top schools in Manchester; Olivia was at the university; I had a job; We had a place of worship. Unbeknown to us, this was just the beginning of God's outpouring of His divine favor. I was having devotion one morning when a verse was illuminated before my eyes and has since become my favorite verse:

> *But as it is written, Eye hath not seen, nor ear heard, neither have entered into the heart of man, the things which God hath prepared for them that love him.*
>
> -1 Corinthians 2:9 (KJV)

A TEST OF COMMITMENT

We surrendered our lives to the will of God. We gave up the comforts of life in Jamaica; I gave up my Job; I left my mother, other family members, and friends behind. We risked it all to follow God's plan for our lives. The journey was never easy, but by God's grace, He gave us the victory!

It is easy following Jesus when life runs smoothly; however, trials reveal our real commitment to Him. Jesus assured us that trials would come to His followers (John 16:33). Discipleship demands sacrifice and Jesus never hid that cost. In Luke 9:57-62, three people seemed willing to follow Jesus. When Jesus questioned them, their commitment was half-hearted at best. They failed to count the cost of following Him. None was willing to take up his cross and crucify self-interest. Therefore, Jesus appeared to dissuade them.[48]

"What is the level of your commitment to God?" How many people would respond to an altar call that went, "Come follow Jesus, and you may face the loss of friends, family, reputation, career, and possibly even your life." If you wonder if you are ready to take up your cross, consider these questions:

- Are you willing to follow Jesus if it means alienation from your family?

- Are you willing to follow Jesus if it means losing some of your closest friends?
- Are you willing to follow Jesus if it means giving up your worldly possessions?
- Are you willing to follow Jesus if it means the loss of your reputation?
- Are you willing to follow Jesus if it means losing your job?
- Are you willing to follow Jesus if it means losing your life?

In some places around the world, these consequences are real. But notice the questions are phrased, "Are you willing?" Following Jesus doesn't necessarily mean all these things will happen to you, but are you willing to take up your cross daily? If there comes a point in your life where you are faced with a choice—Jesus or the comforts of this life—which will you choose?[49]

Commitment to Christ means taking up your cross daily, giving up your hopes, dreams, possessions, even your very life if required for the cause of Christ. Only if you willingly take up your cross may you be called His disciple (Luke 14:27). [50]

Jesus followed His call of death to self ("Take up your cross and follow me") with the gift of life in Christ: "For whoever wants to save his life will lose it, but whoever loses his life for me will find it" (Matthew 16:25-26). What good is it for a man to gain the whole world and lose or forfeit his soul?" (Luke 9:24-25).

Wherever Jesus went, He drew crowds. When Jesus began teaching that He was going to die at the hands of the Jewish leaders (Luke 9:22), His popularity sank. Many of the shocked followers rejected Him. Indeed, they couldn't put to death their ideas, plans, and desires, and exchange them for His. [51]

Jesus said to his disciples, "A disciple is not above his teacher, nor a slave above his master, if they have called the head of the house Beelzebub, how much more the members of his household!" (Mathew 10: 24–25). Christ was saying to His disciples that if He, their Lord, would have to "suffer many things ... and be killed" (Matthew 16:21), how could they expect to escape the same treatment?

Peter also wrote to his fellow believers concerning this matter. "Do not be surprised at the fiery ordeal among you, which comes upon you for your testing, as though some strange thing were happening to you; but to the degree that you share the sufferings of Christ, keep on rejoicing; so that also at the revelation of His glory, you may rejoice with exultation. If you are reviled for the name of Christ, you are blessed, because the Spirit of glory and of God rests upon you" (1 Peter 4:12–14).

My friend, denying yourself, taking up your cross daily and following Jesus will be the best decision you'll ever make. Although the call is tough, the rewards are match-less in this life and for all eternity. You can miss everything in life but don't miss this crucial calling by Jesus. I pray the Lord gives you the grace and wisdom to respond appropri-ately.

~PART THREE~

LIVING THE VICTORIOUS LIFE

CHAPTER ELEVEN

THE DILIGENT SEEKER GETS THE REWARD

"Stick to a task, 'til it sticks to you. Beginners are
many, finishers are few."[52]
— Marjorie Pay Hinckley

*I*F YOU WANT SOMETHING OUT OF LIFE YOU HAVE NEVER had, you must do something you have never done! Many people are guilty of being excited about a project at the start, but later lose interest because they don't see immediate results. Others might be inconsistent in their approach and don't get rewarded because they aren't diligent.

The principle of diligence is applicable in the arena of faith. God rewards the diligent person, the person who seeks after Him persistently until they have received the desired outcome. The Bible puts it this way:

107

But without faith it is impossible to please him.
for he that cometh to God must believe that he is,
and that He is a rewarder of them that diligently
seek him."

- Hebrews 11:6 (KJV)

The last verse says that God is a rewarder of those who diligently seek Him - not those who just merely seek Him. The word 'diligence' is defined as "faithful or persistent application to one's work or studies." It means refusing to give up or let go, to hold firmly or steadfastly to a purpose despite obstacles, warnings or setbacks.

There is a tenacity that God is looking for in our search for Him, and it requires the application of the principle of diligence. It means God rewards those who seek Him diligently. Diligence connects us, the seekers, to God, the rewarder. [53]

The principle of diligence not only applies in the spiritual realm but is applicable in the physical realm too. Proverbs 10:4 teaches:

He becometh poor that dealeth with a slack
hand: but the hand of the diligent maketh rich."
- Proverbs 10:4 (KJV)

APPLICATION OF THE PRINCIPLE OF DILIGENCE – PRAYER FOR RENTAL ACCOMMODATION

Just by our sheer obedience to God's plan for our lives to leave Jamaica and relocate to the UK, God has rewarded us, sometimes double, triple and even multiple folds! God is not a debtor to any man! The Bible confirms this in Mathew 19:29:

> And everyone that hath forsaken houses, or brethren, or sisters, or father, or mother, or wife, or children, or lands, for my name's sake, shall receive a hundredfold, and shall inherit everlasting life.
>
> - Matthew 19:29 (KJV)

I remember seeking the Lord continuously for a rental property, for school for Jordanne and a job. God answered my prayers by closing doors that were not His best and opening those He desired for us. However, the sale of our house in Jamaica remained a stressful situation. A transaction that begun in November with expectation for completion three months later dragged on for a whole year due to numerous complications and setbacks. While I was grateful for my job, there were certain things I couldn't accomplish that year. I continued to pray for the Lord to expedite the sale of our house. Again, because the transaction dragged on for so long, I had to defer my studies for another year.

I was also praying for a house to purchase in the UK. I thank God for our rental property. However, I was tired of living in rentals with the constant barrage of home inspections to assure the landlord the house was being maintained properly.

Our six-month rental agreement was close to expiration, and I decided not to renew my contract due to several plumbing related issues. I started praying and searching for rental properties two months before the end of my contract. I thank God for friends at work, particularly Dominique who drove me to view potential properties. I eventually settled for a rental property close to work, but the property was not ideal, lacking proximity to local shops and transportation points. I was also skeptical whether a three-bedroom, one-bathroom house could accommodate four of us and our furniture from Jamaica. Since I didn't find any other home that was ideal, I decided to settle for this house. Of course, I should have known better! Olivia continually reminds me never to settle for less than God's best. I had doubts about this rental, yet I settled and went ahead with the negotiations.

One week before the end of my existing rental agreement, the new rental fell through the cracks. Again, I found myself in a conundrum, desperately looking for somewhere to live. I prayed, and I searched. A day later, I found a four-bedroom, two-bathroom rental with a private study on three floors. The house came on the market the day I began my frantic search for another property. Wow! Coincidental some people would say, but I say God was at work, yet again!

I didn't drive so it would have been difficult for me to view this new rental property. Holly, another friend at work, was heading in the same direction as the new rental and offered to take me to see the property. It was another well-timed occurrence as Holly typically drives in the opposite direction to get to her home. I viewed the property, fell in love with its spaciousness, and the best part was the rent was less than the previous rental. The agents were aware of my current situation, and they expedited the paperwork to enable us to move in at the appointed time. I was extremely grateful.

The favor of the Lord! I tell you. His goodness knows no bounds! The experience of God working in our lives has now taught me to recognize that closed doors are often for our good. God closes those doors that are not His best and opens the best doors for His children. What a God we serve! Our new rental property was excellent, central and within walking distance from restaurants, supermarkets, hospital, library, bus and train stations. Precisely as we needed it since I didn't drive.

The new rental property met all our needs and housed our furniture quite well. When Olivia came home from university, she was amazed at the spaciousness of the house and excitedly said, "the Lord has moved us from a bungalow in Jamaica to a three-storey house in the UK, a threefold increase." What a God! We sought after Him diligently, and He gave us the desire of our heart (Psalm 37:4).

APPLICATION OF THE PRINCIPLE OF DILIGENCE – PRAYER FOR UNIVERSITY SELECTION

Briana and Jordanne settled very quickly at the new school. Briana was in lower six-form, and as usual, she was off to an excellent start. Her grades were exceptional, and after one month of being in lower six-form, the school placed her in the talented & gifted program. I had initially thought her resentment with our migration plan would affect her school work. However, she continued to apply herself diligently to her work. Over time, our relationship improved as she began to relax and slowly accept the changes.

I continued to pray for Briana concerning her university selection and kept reiterating that she was going to the University of Cambridge. It was the vision I wrote for Briana before leaving Jamaica. We selected the top universities in the UK with the number one choice being, - The University of Cambridge. We continued to pray. I noticed Briana was drawing closer to God, spending more time in His word. God favored all my children in various ways. But I believe God favored Briana in the area she was most diligent - her studies.

The only concern about university education in the UK was that one had to be resident three years before enrolment for local fees to apply. Briana didn't qualify for residency status. Our options were for Briana to take a gap year (a year off) to become eligible or pay international fees. Paying international fees for Olivia and Briana at the same time would not have been ideal, given my financial situation.

Her teacher and a friend advised us that it may be best for Briana to take a gap year. Briana was adamant she wasn't taking a gap year as it would mean being setback for two years. Frankly, I didn't want her to take a gap year, repeating lower six-form was enough. We continued to pray about the situation.

Given my vision for Briana to attend the University of Cambridge, I reluctantly acceded to her request to apply to universities in the USA. She convinced me it would open her prospects for scholarships. Briana then decided to take the Scholastic Aptitude Test (SAT), a test extensively used for college admissions in the USA.

She began her preparation for the SAT in August that year for exams in December. She was constantly studying for the SAT while concurrently preparing for her school exams. She took the SAT and came out with almost perfect scores for more than one module. I was blown away by her results! Her first utterance was, "Yes! Thank you, Jesus!" Afterward, we began the tedious process of applying to schools in the USA. Briana felt that if she were leaving the UK to attend university in the USA, then her sacrifice would only be worthwhile if she got accepted into the top universities in the USA. We narrowed the choices down to two schools - Massachusetts Institute of Technology (MIT) and Harvard University.

In the interim, Briana attended interviews at the University of Cambridge and two other schools in the UK, while awaiting offers from the universities in the US. Shortly afterward, we received the results - Rejection from the University of Cambridge, and acceptance into three of her five UK choices. We were devastated! But I encouraged her to continue to pray. God will work it out for her good. Briana wasn't interested in attending any of the other three UK universities, so we continued to pray that the Lord will grant her the desires of her heart and grant my wish not to place undue stress on my finances.

I believe Briana secretly wanted an offer from MIT given its prestigious status and arguably the number one school in the world. I constantly reiterated that she would need nothing less than full scholarship because I couldn't afford US university fees. I realized we needed a financial miracle as these fees could be quite exorbitant, in the region of seventy thousand dollars or more per year. I continued to pray earnestly, and the Holy Spirit told me to sow a special seed. There was no hesitation on my part, and I enquired as to the amount, heard the value and sowed the seed to the local church in expectation of a great harvest.

In February 2017, Briana received notification of her acceptance into MIT. Wow! We all danced and praised God for the mighty outpouring of His blessings, while we waited for His divine financial favour. Months later, Briana received another notification from MIT informing her of the full scholarship award. We serve a Mighty God indeed! A God who provides for all our needs according to His riches in glory! We are still speechless by His incredible goodness towards us! This was not a triple financial blessing; this was multiple folds! His Word says:

> *Bring ye all the tithes into the storehouse, that there may be meat in mine house, and prove me now herewith, saith the Lord of hosts, if I will not open you the windows of heaven, and pour you out a blessing, that there shall not be room enough to receive it.*
>
> - Malachi 3:10 (KJV)

We couldn't have orchestrated this plan ourselves, only God's supernatural power brought this dream to fruition. God certainly rewarded Briana's diligence and our continued and persistence prayer for His financial blessing. God closed the door to the University of Cambridge, the #2 school to open the door to the #1 University in the World - MIT, and with a full scholarship. Oh! Glory to God from whom all Blessings flow! Only the best is good enough for His children!

APPLICATION OF THE PRINCIPLE OF DILIGENCE – PRAYER FOR A HOME

I mentioned earlier that I was praying for a house to purchase in the UK. I looked for over a year and couldn't find anything that met my expectations. I had a vision of the ideal layout. Eventually, I found a new home, but it didn't quite meet my expectation, so I decided that I wasn't going to waste my time viewing it. The next day, in the middle of my nap, I had a dream that someone was providing me with a tour of a new home, and showed me a beautiful study, which had lovely furniture. I arose from the dream, got dressed and went to view the new home. The house didn't have the study I saw in my dreams; nevertheless, I included my name on a long waiting list. I was still dissatisfied with the new house layout, so I continued my search for other properties.

I came across another new property, but it still didn't meet all my expectations. Unlike the previous property where I had to include my name on a list, the process was 'first come, first serve.' The sales agent told me I would probably need to get to the location by 4.00 am to be first in line when the new homes were released. "What did I do you may ask?" The following week, I took a taxi and got to the location by 5.00 am only to find two cars parked outside waiting for releases. I knew this house didn't meet my exact specification and I continued to pray to the Lord, asking Him to close the door if this wasn't His best. I camped outside the agent's office until it opened at 11 a.m. Shortly after, I received the disappointing news – no home releases that week.

The following week I devised a plan to get to the location the night before so that I could be ahead of other persons. Holly, my friend from work, drove me to the place and I was first in line. I spent the whole night in Holly's car, waiting and praying and asking God to close the door if this wasn't the right house. The Lord surely heard me! The next morning there were no releases! The final straw that broke the camel's back - I just never went back.

My friends, Holly, Dominique, and Cristina were very disappointed with the entire process and they tried their best to encourage me. I continued to pray, asking the Lord why it was so difficult finding a home that met my exact specification. I heard the Lord respond, asking me to specify my requirements. I drew the layout of the house and spoke to God about my needs.

A week later, Dominique drew my attention to a very nice area in Manchester. I then found several new homes in that area. I did some investigation online and viewed the houses. There was one that met my exact specification but was no longer available. I was disappointed! One week later, I felt the Holy Spirit nudging me to call the sales agent. I called, and to my surprise, the builder had just released the house I desired. I couldn't view the exact home, but I saw a show home similar in size and that was enough for me to begin the process of purchasing our new house. The process was hassle free, no first come first serve, and no long waiting list.

The sale of our house in Jamaica was completed just in time to pay the deposit for our new home and to take a trip to visit my mother in Jamaica. God is indeed amazing! His timing is perfect! Now we await our new home, a home with the ideal layout, inclusive of a study. Hallelujah to the Almighty God! There is no one like you! We sold our house and possessions in Jamaica, and God restored everything! Restoration for God means to return more than what has been lost, stolen or given up, with the final state of the person being greater than the original state (Joel 2:25). Oh, glory to God! You are indeed a Restorer!

APPLICATION OF THE PRINCIPLES OF DILIGENCE – DRAWING CLOSER TO GOD

Over the past 14 years, I have desired to draw closer to God and to seek His will for my life. Being in the UK has been lonely at times without those familiar faces we left behind in Jamaica. However, I used the opportunity to draw closer to God by continuously reading my Bible and praying.

During the period when I was at home and actively seeking employment, the Holy Spirit gave me the idea of writing this book on faith. As I fashioned the pages of this book, I continued to receive revelations from the Holy Spirit on the content. Again! I had another dream.

Seventh Dream

In this dream, I saw a golden ark of the covenant coming down from the clouds into my bedroom. I saw an angel, and he asked me where I wanted him to put the ark, at the foot of my bed or outside in the corridor. I responded, "at the foot of my bed." I was asked whether I wanted a spiritual ark or a physical ark, and I answered, "a spiritual ark." I awoke from the dream and was instantly reassured of God's abiding presence, giving me an unshakeable confidence in Him. I know God will always take care of us despite life's challenges.

I thank God for allowing me to write this book on faith. I have now given birth to my first book after almost three years of diligently prodding. I believe Book two will be completed in the fullness of God's time. I have grown closer to God since writing this book. I have gained wonderful insights about God and recognized how He ordered our steps. I can now truly say, "It was good to have been afflicted," If I hadn't been afflicted, I wouldn't know God as a provider, a way maker, a healer, a protector, and a restorer. I give Him all the praise and Glory due to His Mighty Name! God is indeed a rewarder of those who diligently seek him!

I recognize now that faith in God doesn't become stronger during times of peace and tranquility, but it is in times of trouble our faith grows, and God operates mightily to deliver us. Therefore, "…. Yea, though I walk through the valley of the shadow of death, I will fear no evil: for thou art with me; thy rod and thy staff they comfort me" (Psalm 23:4).

Whatever situation you are faced with today, talk to God in prayer about it. God isn't oblivious to what is happening in your life. God is with you. Trust in Him to deliver you, and while you wait for your deliverance, obey His instruction to you. God never promised a life of immunity against trials and tribulations, but He will cause all things to work together for your good, to them that love God and are called according to His purposes (Romans 8:28).

OTHER EXAMPLES OF DILIGENCE IN ACTION

Successful people know what it means to practice the principle of diligence - to regularly, continuously and persistently undertake a task until they have achieved the desired results. If diligence is guaranteed to work in the natural realm, imagine the effects of consistent, continuous and tireless application to one's work or studies in the spiritual realm. Jesus taught the following parable about diligence in Luke 11: 5:

> Then He said to them, "Suppose one of you has a friend, and goes to him at midnight and says to him, 'Friend, lend me three loaves; for a friend of mine has come to me from a journey, and I have nothing to set before him'; and from inside he answers and says, 'Do not bother me; the door has

already been shut and my children and I are in
bed; I cannot get up and give you anything.' "I tell
you, even though he will not get up and give him
anything because he is his friend, yet because of
his persistence he will get up and give him as
much as he needs.

- Luke 11: 5-8 (KJV)

The last sentence explains that the man will not rise because the man asking for help is his friend. It is somewhat ironic because you would expect the verse to read, "Because he is my friend I will rise and give him what he wants." Likewise, God says that He will not answer you just because you are His child.[54]

The word "yet" in the last verse brings out the diligence of the man seeking bread for his guests. The verse reads "yet because of his "persistence," but it could also read "yet because of his shameless persistence, and diligence." The man in need was shamelessly persistent, and because of this, his friend got up and gave him as much as he needed. If he had knocked once, he would have gone home with no bread. He did not receive the bread just because that man was his friend; he received the bread because of his shameless insistence.

Likewise, God expects diligence, a consistent, continuous and tireless knocking at His door by you until He answers your prayers. You must get to the point where you're not ashamed anymore. You must insist that God answer you. God will not answer you just because you are His child. He will answer you because of your shameless insistence, persistence, and diligence. Don't give up! [55]

While God rewards the diligent seeker, you cannot, however, expect God to reward your diligence if you are not God's child. Firstly, you must be a child of God (believe that He is God) and you must believe that He is a rewarder of those who diligently seek Him. Jesus illustrates the principle of diligence in the following verses:

> *And I say unto you, Ask, and it shall be given you; seek and ye shall find; knock, and it shall be opened unto you. For everyone that asketh receiveth; and he that seeketh findeth; and to him that knocketh it shall be opened."*
>
> - Luke 11: 9-10 (KJV)

Diligence requires you to ask God and keep on asking; seek and keep on seeking and knock and keep knocking loudly and boldly until the door is opened unto you. God is not always going to answer you the first time you knock. God only rewards the resolute seeker. God will stir himself up on your behalf if you seek Him diligently. He will move heaven and earth if that's what it takes to solve your problems. Seek God diligently, and He will answer diligently.[56]

In Luke 18:1-8, Jesus teaches His disciples what it means not to faint, lose heart and give up. He says men ought always to pray and not faint. The parable illustrated describes an unjust judge who neither feared God nor man. There was a widow who solicited him to avenge her of her adversary, but he would not honor her request. However, since she diligently and persistently pursued the judge, he finally decided to hear her case and grant her request. The woman wearied the judge. She would not give up. She did not lose heart. She did not faint. The judge finally judged her case in her favor.

That's what God wants you to do. He wants you to be persistent. God only rewards diligence. If diligence changes an evil judge, surely it will change God. It seems God purposely holds back to see if you will come after Him. Most of the time there's a waiting period. But remember, only the seeker who is consistent and persistent gets the reward.

The story of Naaman in the Bible (2 Kings 5) is another example of a resolute seeker. Naaman had leprosy and received instructions to dip seven times in the muddy Jordan River. God knew that if Naaman was told to dip seven times that would be a test of his tenacity. God healed Naaman after he took the seventh dip. What would have happened had he stopped after the first or second or third dip? He wouldn't have received his healing.[57]

What are you prepared to do as the seeker to get the reward from the rewarder? Are you ready to go to any lengths to get God's attention and your reward? Do you need healing today? Are there impossible situations that you need to overcome? Now ask yourself whether you are diligently seeking after God. Are you seeking first the kingdom of God and His righteousness (Matthew 6:33)? Are you taking up your cross daily and following Christ (Matthew 14:24)?

God does not want you to give up. He wants you to keep knocking. Remain steadfast even in the face of refusal. Press toward the mark of the prize of the high calling, and you will not miss your reward. Remember, diligence hooks the seeker with the rewarder. [58]

Beloved, when you diligently come to the Lord with your needs, believe that He is God and that He is a rewarder. God has pleasure in this kind of diligent faith. He wants to be the rewarder of your faith in Him![59] Today, I urge you to seek God diligently. The faith that pleases God is the kind of diligent faith that believes God exists and He is a rewarder of those who diligently seek Him.

CHAPTER TWELVE

FAITH IS THE VICTORY

*"This is what the past is for! Every experience
God gives us, every person He puts in our lives is
the perfect preparation for the future that only
He can see."* [60]
— *Corrie ten Boom, Hiding Place*

*I*NDEED, FAITH IS THE VICTORY! GOD'S WORD HAS produced faith in us, and the outcome is the victory. God acted mightily on our behalf because we chose to trust and obey Him, sacrificing the comforts of life and the embrace of familiarity to venture into the unknown. We risked it all for a known God, and He rewarded our faith exceedingly above and beyond our wildest imaginations! Everything we gave up to follow God's plan for our lives, He gave back to us multiple folds! God led us by dreams and covered us every step of the way. Every dream was made manifest and came to past.

My first dream alluded to an unknown destination, which in hindsight we know was the UK. I saw an empty house in my third dream, and indeed the house in Jamaica was empty either from selling, shipping or giving away the contents of our home. Sending some of our furniture to the UK saved us a fortune and spared us the expense of purchasing huge amounts of furnishings for our new home. Every dream I received from God came to past, not as I expected, but as He orchestrated it.

We placed our trust in God, and the outcome has been greater than we could ever imagine! Every difficult experience that tried to break our resolve in believing God was turned around into a victory celebration. God used the difficult moments to teach us many invaluable lessons. Every closed door was for our good, and God led us to the open doors - His best. Like a jigsaw puzzle, our steps were being ordered by the Lord. To God be the Glory, great things He has done!

The Bible teaches us that our faith is the victory. It says:

> *For this demonstrates our love for God: We keep his commandments, and his commandments are not difficult, because everyone who is born from God has overcome the world. Our faith is the victory that overcomes the world.*
>
> - John 5:3-4 (ISV)

Faith is the victory is a well-known verse, but sometimes its interpretation tends to skew its meaning. We believe that it is faith that carries us into victory. However, if you reread the verse, it says our faith is the victory. By merely paraphrasing the verse 'our faith is the victory' to include the definition of faith, which comes by hearing and hearing by the word of God, we can say that "our hearing and acting on God's word is the victory." Hence "our faith in God is the victory." [61]

When we put our faith in God, it is evidence that God has gotten His way with us – We have seen the truth, and we have embraced it. In other words, the existence of faith in us is evidence of God's victory in us. When God has full victory over us, and His victory is established in us through our relationship with Him - then this is faith, and this faith is His victory.[62]

What all of this means is quite simple - Victory is not a thing, it is a Person. The Person is Jesus Christ, and when Jesus has full victory as Lord over us – then we can live in and move in His victory over all of life's circumstances. Jesus said, "These things I have spoken unto you, that in me ye might have peace. In the world ye shall have tribulation: but be of good cheer; I have overcome the world" (John 16:33). Because Jesus has overcome the world, by putting our faith in Him, we too have overcome the world. That is why faith in God is the victory that overcomes the world!

LOOKING THROUGH THE LENS OF MY PAST

I can't begin to share how overwhelmed I am by God's goodness and divine favour. Words cannot do justice to His grace, mercy and love towards us. When I look back over the years, I recognized how God has ordered our steps. The Bible says:

> *The steps of a good man are ordered by the Lord:*
> *and he delighteth in his way.*
> - Psalm 37:23 (KJV)

When my marriage ended, I thought my world had shattered, while in fact, it was a blessing in disguise. It was the catalyst that led all of us to Jesus Christ. God indeed makes all things, both good and bad, work together for good to them that love Him. I asked God to rescue my family, and He did. Now, regardless of what happens in life, we know we are safe in Him, and our eternal destination is secure.

I remember the times when I was trying to sell all my work attire as I felt I was immediately going to pursue further studies in the UK. Of the work suits I possessed, only five sold. I tried every avenue to sell the others but to no avail. Again, that was God closing those doors! Now I understand why - I am currently wearing the same clothes to work. What a predicament, if I had sold all of them! Furthermore, it would have cost me a fortune to replace them. I am so glad God closed those doors. The plans to pursue further studies are still in place and will be accomplished in the fullest of God's timing.

I look back at the moment when I was trying to purchase another house in Jamaica, and every deal fell through. I applied twice to my company for a house loan, asking for concessions each time to qualify for the loan. After five years of searching, I found a house, which I could only afford, after selling my existing home. The house needed much work, and I was willing to undertake the renovations. I began the process to buy the house, but the seller refused to lower her price within my budget, so the deal fell through again.

It was not long afterward, that I began to receive those dreams from God. I see now why God closed those doors; He had already prepared a plan of immigration to the UK. It would have been difficult to have recently purchased another house, tied myself to a huge mortgage and then try to sell the house in a short space of time. It would also have tied up the resources we needed to immigrate to the UK.

At the time, I was disappointed the deal fell through, but in hindsight, I am glad God closed the door and opened the door to our beautiful home in the UK. I am elated I didn't hold onto the house in Jamaica when God had a better one in store for us, with a layout that matched my exact specification. Thank you, Jesus! God is not a debtor to any man, indeed!

In my first dream, I mentioned that I saw my friend, Tina from Canada in the dream, but I knew the destination was not Canada. The reason I was so sure was because God had closed that door several years ago when I applied to emigrate to Canada, and my application was rejected. At the time, I didn't realize God was opening the door for migration to the UK. I was so disappointed that I wasn't going to Canada. I didn't pray for days and eventually I had to confess my disappointment to God. I thank God for that closed door.

I reminisce about Briana's attitude towards our migration plans. We now see how God turned her setback into a miraculous setup that has left us still astounded by His favour. But the Lord did promise in His Word;

> But as it is written, Eye hath not seen, nor ear heard, neither have entered into the heart of man, the things which God hath prepared for them that love him.
>
> - 1 Corinthians 2: 9 (KJV)

God's divine favour is so huge, I believe it will change the trajectory of our future generation, even to the 10th generation. I recognized from Briana's experience that sometimes the most potent, effective and beneficial thing

one can do to catapult forward is to take a step back. I
thank God she eventually obeyed Him because it was her
setback God used to launch her into a marvelous destiny.
If we had remained in Jamaica for the sake of Briana, she
may not have received acceptance into MIT, and oh what a
missed opportunity that would have been! I prayed for better prospects for my children, and God answered my
prayer in a mighty way. Olivia is in London, doing well at
the university and Jordanne is doing fine in secondary
school. I am so glad we put our trust in God; He alone
knows the future.

When my application for study-leave was rejected,
that was God, at work again, closing those doors. Even if I
had received the study-leave, the funds wouldn't have
been enough to cover my needs and Olivia's international
fees. The study-leave grant would have restricted my ef-
forts in obtaining full time employment. I don't know how
we would have survived if I hadn't sought employment
given our house in Jamaica didn't sell at the expected time.
Looking back now, I thank God the head of the area didn't
grant the study leave. At the time I was disappointed, but
God turned it around for my good. Now, I can say it was
good to have been afflicted, had I not been afflicted, I
wouldn't have realized God's best for our lives.

Several persons have marveled at the way God has
worked in our lives. My longtime friend Judith, who was
very worried about my resignation from my company and

my relocation with no job and three children to feed, has been utterly amazed at how God has worked mightily in our lives. Based on our story, she has now developed a renewed confidence in God. Her desire now is to grow closer to Him. I give God the praise and the Glory for transforming the life of my friend.

The Lord continues to order our footsteps. We continue to fight the good fight of faith and lay hold on His every promise despite the challenges. After all, He is our present help in times of trouble; He is the father to the fatherless, and He is mighty and powerful!

There are so many lessons I have learned on this journey of faith. More importantly, I have developed a renewed faith and confidence in God. Other powerful lessons are listed below in no particular order:

- Honor the Lord, with your heart, mind, body, soul and your finances;
- Never settle for less than God's best;
- Be quick to obey the voice of God;
- Ask God for little things but don't be afraid to ask for impossible things;
- When you make your request known to God, be specific about it;
- God is not afraid of desperate prayers; remind Him of His promises;

- A closed door is God's way of leading you to the open door He has prepared. Don't get bitter, don't quit and Praise God Always;
- No form of protection is as good as the protection from the Almighty God;
- His presence is forever with those who love Him;
- He is the greatest lover of our soul;
- His goodness knows no bounds, and He surprises in ways one least expects;
- He answers prayers, some immediately, some months after, some many years after. Be persistent! He will respond, and His timing is always perfect; and
- In all things, and in all seasons, give God the glory, honor, and praise that is due to His Mighty Name.

FAST FORWARD INTO THE FUTURE

While I was completing this book, it occurred to me that the seventh dream had not come to pass. In the seventh dream, I saw myself in an advanced state of pregnancy emerging out of parked cars on the streets in the UK. I decided to ask God about the dream. The Lord answered my question by showing me what was happening.

Eighth Dream

In this dream, I saw myself looking in a room where a lady was lying on a table about to give birth. What struck me about the dream was that she was surrounded by evil forces who had towels waiting to steal the child as it came forth out of the mother's womb. I peered closer to see who this woman was - surprisingly it was me! I awoke out of the dream startled and began praying to the Lord about the dream and its implications. I realized why I hadn't given birth; the timing was not right. God revealed what was happening. Evil forces were trying to steal the dream. My response was to pray for God to arise and, ".... let His enemies be scattered: let them also that hate Him flee before Him" (Psalm 68:1)

One year later, I had another dream. This time I was in a hospital room. I gave birth to twins, then unawares to everyone around, I gave birth to triplets. The nurse came into my room and was startled when she saw the triplets and enquire when it happened.

I arose from my dream and prayed, asking the Holy Spirit about the twin and the triplet mission.

Mission Revealed

It was sometime afterward that the Holy Spirit revealed to me that part of the twin mission was the book I was writing. The other part concerned caring for orphans, widows, fatherless, strangers and the homeless in Manchester and the nation at large. I am not surprised by this mission. When I came to Manchester, I was shocked to see the number of homeless people, sleeping rough on the streets. It pained my heart, and I carried a burden ever since to help eradicate homelessness.

According to the statutory definition of homelessness, we would have been classified as homeless, living in hotels for almost two weeks when we came to Manchester. I recall going to the Manchester council to see if they could assist us in finding suitable accommodation. I had the funds to pay, and I thought they could provide us with a quick solution, but that was not the case. We later checked out of the expensive hotel and found a taxi owner who helped us locate a reasonably priced hotel. Eventually, we found the furnished rental in Old Trafford. I realize many people are not as privileged to find, and afford suitable accommodation, and my heart bleeds for them.

The mission to rescue the orphans, widows, fatherless, strangers and the homeless has been birthed. The heart of God is to restore men and women to their rightful place in Him, and I am humbled to be used by Him in this mighty way. God has given me some ideas which I have turned into a proposal. My second book will speak more about this mission.

The triplet mission has already begun in earnest. Unbeknown to me, the Lord connected me to three beautiful young ladies whom I met at my workplace. I am truly grateful for their assistance over the last two years. When I was looking for a rental; looking to purchase a house; celebrating Briana's achievement; they were all there. I have adopted them as my children, and I continue to invest in their lives. I hold them accountable for the goals and dreams God has placed within them. I give God thanks for Cristina, Holly, and Dominique. I hope that they come to know God as their Lord and Savior. I continue to pray for them as I pray for my children.

Living a life of daily trusting God is a life full of adventure. I await the next phase of our lives and what God has in store.

FINAL WORDS

IT'S YOUR TIME NOW!

*"Risk an unknown future to a known God, you
will be surprised what you find."*
— *Bosede Nelson*

*B*USINESS PEOPLE KNOW THAT WITHOUT RISK
there can be no rewards. They set both short- and
long-range goals to increase their rewards while trying to
minimize any risk or uncertainty that might derail their
progress. Because life is full of uncertainties, even the best-
laid plans are not guaranteed to work. Likewise, as individuals, we have dreams of achieving great success, but it may
or may not materialize because we don't know what the
future holds.

No human being knows what the future holds, but God
does! Therefore, when you put your trust in God, the risk
about the future turns into complete assurance because

God holds the future in His hands. He is the perfect navigator and compass to guide you through life. He knows your end from your beginning. Before you were formed in the womb, "I knew you," says the Lord, "before you were born I set you apart; I appointed you as a prophet to the nations" (Jeremiah 1:5). He is also your bodyguard and spiritual guide. When He guards you, no harm can befall you (Psalm 91:3-11) because His power is unstoppable and above every power conceivable! (Ephesians 1:21)

An out of the box thinker, we cannot comprehend God's ways, His methods are unknowable, and His thoughts are unsearchable. But one thing I know is that His thoughts towards you are to prosper and not to harm you, to give you a hope and a future (Jeremiah 29:11). God knows the purpose for your existence, and He has a perfect plan for your life. God has wonderfully and marvelously designed you to accomplish that plan or purpose He has placed inside of you. God is more than capable of helping you realize your purpose. Do not leave this earth until you have accomplished everything you were created to do!

Our story has been one of love, grace, forgiveness and unmerited favor. I ran to God because I couldn't navigate life on my own. No one can! I thank God for Jesus! I now live a life full of intrigue, excitement and sheer unadulterated joy, which trumps moments of frustration, pain, and disappointment that comes with life itself. More importantly, our eternal destination is secure in God.

Now it's your time to shake off everything that has held you back. No matter what the situation is today, call out to God to help you. He knows what is happening to you right now. God is not asleep on the job. He also knows your past and your future. God knows who has hurt, disappointed, and rejected you. He knows about the illness, your job situation, and that family issue. His response to you is to cast all your worries and cares on Him because He cares for you (1 Peter 5:7). God wants you to exchange those burdens you carry for His love, joy, peace, grace, and forgiveness. He wants to give you an abundant life on earth, and eternal life with Him after this life on earth is over. Let God help you break off the shackles that are holding you back from living your best life.

He is calling you to come to Him just as you are. God wants to have a relationship with you. He wants to restore you and do a marvelous thing in your life. No sin is too great that He cannot forgive, no prayer too difficult that He cannot answer, and no situation too grave that He cannot resolve. He is Almighty God, the one who put the sun, the stars and the moon in place; there is nothing too hard for Him to do! He is calling you today to come as you are. Run to the Father, who wants to love you and show you how a good Father treats His children. The Bible says:

That if you confess with your mouth Jesus as Lord, and believe in your heart that God raised Him from the dead, you will be saved;

- Romans 10:9 (NAS)

When you have accepted Jesus Christ as your Lord and Savior, the abundant life awaits you! A life of victory designed to catapult you into destiny while overcoming every challenging situation. Conscious of your loving Father's acceptance and approval, you will soar on eagles' wings when you apprehend, by faith, the inexhaustible riches of His grace.

Don't waste any more time! Don't settle for less than God's best; the victorious life awaits you! Destiny has come knocking, will you answer the door! I pray God gives you the courage to open the door to a life of love, favor, grace, abundant life and victorious living!

As I close this book, I declare that our latter years shall be greater than the former; I declare that our children shall be mighty in this land, and I declare that we shall live and not die to declare the Works of the Lord and to proclaim the MIGHTY NAME OF JESUS.

I hope this book has helped you to realize that nothing is impossible with God. Accept Him as your Lord and Savior, believe in Him, and He will reward you if you diligently seek Him. By choosing God, you have chosen the path of victory! I pray that your story and testimony will far exceed the experiences documented in this book.

To God be the Glory Forever and Ever! Amen.

ACKNOWLEDGEMENTS

I WANT TO THANK MY MOTHER, ROWENA FOR HER LOVE and support over the years and her help in supporting my children. I am grateful to my children, Olivia, Briana, and Jordanne for their love and support during the months it took to write this book. To Patricia Rose, I thank you for your friendship, encouragement, support and Godly advice throughout our faith journey. For editorial assistance, I thank Patricia Rose and Jeneive Gordon.

I'm grateful to Pastor Spencer Colquhoun, the rest of the leadership and the members of the Portmore Missionary Church in Jamaica for all their prayers and support. I am grateful to Senior Pastor, Barrington Mullings, and Mrs. Maxine Mullings, the rest of the leadership and the members of the New Testament Church of God, Brooks Bar, for their prayers and welcoming support into our new church home.

There are so many others to thank that have made a difference in our lives. I'm grateful to my brothers, Abiodun Nelson and Wale Nelson and their wives, Akos, and Christine for their support. To my adopted daughters, Holly Woodside-Coventry, Dominique Lambert and Cristina Dominte whose kindness knows no bounds. I am grateful to Professor Claremont Kirton and Courtney Allen who believed in me and signed numerous documents concerning my university applications.

I am grateful to my former coworkers, Judith Bailey-Edwards, Ernestine Jaggon-Fraser, Robert Stennett, Tanisha Ennis, Sharon Miller-Betty, Hilary Robertson, and Chevanese Morais who supported us over the years. I thank specific members of my church family in Jamaica, Annmarie Prendergast, Roberta Daley, 'Storyteller' Clarke, and Tonelle Beecher for their faith in us; and my friend, Angela McGowan for her continued and unwavering support of the entire family and her present support for my mother.

It has been an honor being a part of the Signature Gatekeepers' Ministry, and I'm grateful to Lameta Lugg and the rest of the Signature Gatekeepers for their unceasing prayers and support.

Finally, I thank God for the favor He granted my children during their secondary school years. I am grateful to Mrs. Sharon Reid, Principal, St. Andrew High School for girls and to Mrs. Grace Baston, Principal, Campion College.

Last but by no means least, I am truly grateful to the Director of Sixth Form, Mr. Mike Dore and the entire staff at Parrs Wood High School for their incredible support and for believing in my children. May the Lord bless and prosper all of you. Amen!

ABOUT THE AUTHOR

*B*OSEDE NELSON IS A CHILD OF GOD AND FOUNDER OF THE BibleCards Ministries, which provides distributional material to aid in the spreading of the gospel. She is also a member of the Signature Gatekeepers, a ministry focused on restoring and empowering women. This book, '*Risk an unknown future to a known God,*' is Bosede's first book, and she has expectations to publish the second part of this book soon. Bosede Nelson lives in Manchester, UK with her children.

If this book has changed your life, please send an email to: Bosede.Nelson8557@gmail.com letting her know how God has transformed your life.

Notes

INTRODUCTION: THE DREAM CHASER

1   Reinhard Bonnke, Quote, //smartandrelentless.com/faith-without-works-is-dead-quotes-by-spirit-filled-leaders/

CHAPTER ONE: SELF VS GOD: THE CONCEPT OF FAITH

2   Germany Kent, Quote: https://www.good-reads.com/quotes/8408819-the-only-way-you-re-going-to-reach-places-you-ve-never

3   Br. David Vryhof, "What It Means to Have Faith in God," Society of St. John the Evangelist, April 7, 2013, https://www.ssje.org/2013/04/07/what-it-means-to-have-faith-in-god-br-david-vryhof/

CHAPTER TWO: FAITH COMES BY HEARING GOD

4   Rick Warren, Quote, https://rickwarrenquotes.blog-spot.com/2014/06/on-hearing-god.html

5   Pastor Glenn Pease, "The Foundation of Faith," Faith Life Sermons, https://sermons.faithlife.com/ser-mons/125346-the-foundation-of-faith

---

CHAPTER 3: THE SUBSTANCE OF THINGS WE DESIRE

6   Corrie Ten Boom, Quotes, https://www.brainyquote.com/quotes/corrie_ten_boom_381184

7   Keith Sharp, "Now Faith Is," June 2012 - http://www.christistheway.com/now-faith-is/

8   Keith Sharp, "Now Faith Is," June 2012 - http://www.christistheway.com/now-faith-is/

9   Keith Sharp, "Now Faith Is," June 2012 - http://www.christistheway.com/now-faith-is/

CHAPTER 4: FAITH WITHOUT ACTION IS DEAD

10   Reinhard Bonnke, Quote, //smartandrelentless.com/faith-without-works-is-dead-quotes-by-spirit-filled-leaders/

11   Worthy Ministries, "Put Your Faith into Action," August 2017, https://www.worthydevotions.com/christian-devotional/put-your-faith-into-action

12   Worthy Ministries, "Put Your Faith into Action," August 2017, https://www.worthydevotions.com/christian-devotional/put-your-faith-into-action

CHAPTER 5: TRUE FAITH IS TRIED AND TESTED

13   George Muller (Evangelist and missionary, Quotes, //smartandrelentless.com/faith-without-works-is-dead-quotes-by-spirit-filled-leaders/

14   Joseph Copeland, "A Faith that Worketh Patience, 2007, https://sermons.faithlife.com/sermons/5195-a-faith-that-worketh-patience

15 Joseph Copeland, "A Faith that Worketh Patience, 2007, https://sermons.faithlife.com/sermons/5195-a-faith-that-worketh-patience

16 Joseph Copeland, "A Faith that Worketh Patience, 2007, https://sermons.faithlife.com/sermons/5195-a-faith-that-worketh-patience

17 Joseph Copeland, "A Faith that Worketh Patience, 2007, https://sermons.faithlife.com/sermons/5195-a-faith-that-worketh-patience

18 Joseph Copeland, "A Faith that Worketh Patience, 2007, https://sermons.faithlife.com/sermons/5195-a-faith-that-worketh-patience

19 Joseph Copeland, "A Faith that Worketh Patience, 2007, https://sermons.faithlife.com/sermons/5195-a-faith-that-worketh-patience

20 Joseph Copeland, "A Faith that Worketh Patience, 2007, https://sermons.faithlife.com/sermons/5195-a-faith-that-worketh-patience

21 Joseph Copeland, "A Faith that Worketh Patience, 2007, https://sermons.faithlife.com/sermons/5195-a-faith-that-worketh-patience

CHAPTER 6: MUSTARD SEED FAITH CAN MOVE MOUNTAINS

22 E.W Kenyon (Pastor), Quotes, //smartandrelentless.com/faith-without-works-is-dead-quotes-by-spirit-filled-leaders/

23 The Church at Asheville, "Mustard Seed Faith," https://www.thechurchatasheville.com/faith/mustard-seed-faith/

24 The Church at Asheville, "Mustard Seed Faith,"
    https://www.thechurchatasheville.com/faith/mustard-
    seed-faith/

25 The Church at Asheville, "Mustard Seed Faith,"
    https://www.thechurchatasheville.com/faith/mustard-
    seed-faith/

26 Small Faith Can Accomplish Great Things,
    https://www.crosswindsinternational.org/wp-con-
    tent/uploads/2017/04/Small-Faith-Can-Accomplish-
    Great-Things.pdf

CHAPTER 7: FORSAKING OTHERS MAY BE NECESSARY

27 Billy Graham, Billy Graham in Quotes, https://www.good-
    reads.com/quotes/tag/discipline?page=11

CHAPTER 8: FAITH STANDS IN THE POWER OF GOD

28 Benson Idahosa (Pentecostal preacher), Quotes, //smar-
    tandrelentless.com/faith-without-works-is-dead-quotes-
    by-spirit-filled-leaders/

29 God Is All-Powerful. http://discovergod.com/charac-
    ter02.html

30 God Is All-Powerful. http://discovergod.com/charac-
    ter02.html

31 God Is All-Powerful. http://discovergod.com/charac-
    ter02.html

32 God Is All-Powerful. http://discovergod.com/charac-
    ter02.html

CHAPTER 9: FIGHT THE GOOD FIGHT OF FAITH

33   Abraham Lincoln, Quotes, https://www.good-reads.com/quotes/38057-i-have-been-driven-many-times-upon-my-knees-by

34   Kingdom CultureNG, "Fighting The Fight- Running The Race," August 2016, http://kingdomcultureng.com/2016/08/17/fighting-the-fight-running-the-race/

35   Kingdom CultureNG, "Fighting The Fight- Running The Race," August 2016, http://kingdomcultureng.com/2016/08/17/fighting-the-fight-running-the-race/

36   Kingdom CultureNG, "Fighting The Fight- Running The Race," August 2016, http://kingdomcultureng.com/2016/08/17/fighting-the-fight-running-the-race/

37   Kingdom CultureNG, "Fighting The Fight- Running The Race," August 2016, http://kingdomcultureng.com/2016/08/17/fighting-the-fight-running-the-race/

38   Rev, Kenneth W. Hagin, Fighting the Fight – Running the Race – Article, ," August 2016, http://www.rhema.org/index.php?option=com_content&view=article&id=240:fighting-the-fight-running-the-race&Itemid=141

39   Rev, Kenneth W. Hagin, Fighting the Fight – Running the Race – Article, ," August 2016, http://www.rhema.org/in-

dex.php?option=com_content&view=arti-
cle&id=240:fighting-the-fight-running-the-
race&Itemid=141

40   Rev, Kenneth W. Hagin, Fighting the Fight – Running the
     Race – Article, ," August 2016, http://www.rhema.org/in-
     dex.php?option=com_content&view=arti-
     cle&id=240:fighting-the-fight-running-the-
     race&Itemid=141 /

41   Sigurd Bratlie, "What does it mean to fight the good fight
     of faith?" https://activechristianity.org/mean-fight-good-
     fight-faith

42   Sigurd Bratlie, "What does it mean to fight the good fight
     of faith?" https://activechristianity.org/mean-fight-good-
     fight-faith

CHAPTER 10: TAKING UP YOUR CROSS DAILY

43   Watchman Nee, (Martyr of Christ), Quotes, http://smar-
     tandrelentless.com/faith-without-works-is-dead-quotes-
     by-spirit-filled-leaders/

44   Bill Mounce, "What does it mean to "deny yourself?" Feb
     2012, https://www.westernseminary.edu/transformed-
     blog/2012/02/09/what-does-it-mean-to-deny-yourself/

45   Bill Mounce, "What does it mean to "deny yourself?" Feb
     2012, https://www.westernseminary.edu/transformed-
     blog/2012/02/09/what-does-it-mean-to-deny-yourself/

46   John Nel, Take Up Your Cross and Follow Me (Article),
     12th December 2016, http://john-
     nel.com/2016/12/12/take-up-your-cross-and-follow-me/

47 John Nel, Take Up Your Cross and Follow Me (Article), 12th December 2016 - http://john-nel.com/2016/12/12/take-up-your-cross-and-follow-me/

48 John Nel, Take Up Your Cross and Follow Me (Article), 12th December 2016, http://john-nel.com/2016/12/12/take-up-your-cross-and-follow-me/

49 John Nel, Take Up Your Cross and Follow Me (Article), 12th December 2016, http://john-nel.com/2016/12/12/take-up-your-cross-and-follow-me/

50 John Nel, Take Up Your Cross and Follow Me (Article), 12th December 2016, http://john-nel.com/2016/12/12/take-up-your-cross-and-follow-me/

51 John Nel, Take Up Your Cross and Follow Me (Article), 12th December 2016 - http://john-nel.com/2016/12/12/take-up-your-cross-and-follow-me/

CHAPTER 11: THE DILIGENT SEEKER GETS THE REWARD

52 Marjorie Pay Hinckley, Small and Simple Things, Quotes, https://www.goodreads.com/quotes/605874-stick-to-a-task-til-it-sticks-to-you-beginners

53 John Museredzo, "7 Biblical Truths for True Leaders"

54 John Museredzo, "7 Biblical Truths for True Leaders"

55 John Museredzo, "7 Biblical Truths for True Leaders"

56 John Museredzo, "7 Biblical Truths for True Leaders"

57 John Museredzo, "7 Biblical Truths for True Leaders"

58 John Museredzo, "7 Biblical Truths for True Leaders"

59 John Museredzo, "7 Biblical Truths for True Leaders"

CHAPTER 12: FAITH IS THE VICTORY

60   Corrie Ten Boom, The Hiding Place, Quotes,
     https://www.goodreads.com/quotes/94188-this-is-what-
     the-past-is-for-every-experience-god

61   David A. DePra, Faith is the Victory (Article)
     http://www.goodnewsarticles.com/May10-1.htm

62   David A. DePra, Faith is the Victory (Article)
     http://www.goodnewsarticles.com/May10-1.htm

NOTES

NOTES

www.ingramcontent.com/pod-product-compliance
Lightning Source LLC
Chambersburg PA
CBHW031845090426
42741CB00005B/353